THE
CHAMPIONSHIPS
WIMBLEDON
Official Annual 1995

JOHN PARSONS

Photographs by
CLIVE BRUNSKILL, GARY M. PRIOR *and* **CLIVE MASON**
of Allsport Photographic

Publisher
RICHARD POULTER

Production Manager
STEVEN PALMER

Business Development Manager
SIMON MAURICE

Art Editor
BOB BICKERTON

Copy Editor
KAY EDGE

Production Controller
CLARE RAGGETT

Photography
CLIVE BRUNSKILL
GARY M. PRIOR
CLIVE MASON

Photo Research, Allsport
ANDREW REDINGTON
ELAINE LOBO

This first edition published in 1995 by Hazleton Publishing Ltd,
3 Richmond Hill, Richmond, Surrey TW10 6RE

ISBN: 1-874557-31-4

Printed in England by Ebenezer Baylis & Son Ltd, Worcester

Colour reproduction by Adroit Photo Litho Ltd, Birmingham

Results tables are reproduced by courtesy of
The All England Lawn Tennis Club

This book is produced with the assistance of Nikon (UK) Limited

FOREWORD

1995 was the year that visitors to Wimbledon saw the first steps of our long-term plan, as the new Court One took shape. It is a major redevelopment, but it did not disturb the serene path of The Championships.

What a vintage year 1995 was: good weather, great tennis and two wonderful champions. It was another happy sunshine Championships, completely rain free. In spite of the blazing sun the grass played beautifully throughout the tournament. The players loved the warmth and the perfect courts.

From the opening match on the Centre Court, we had outstanding tennis and excitement. It was lovely to see the best players performing up to expectation. The top four seeds came through to the semi-finals in both the ladies' and the gentlemen's singles events for the first time ever. However, they only reached their respective semi-finals after some tough competition. Even Pete Sampras, the best player on grass at the moment, had difficult matches before he became champion.

Of course Boris Becker had that epic quarter-final against Cedric Pioline which lasted four-and-a-quarter hours, and success was only achieved after being 2–4 down in the final set.

But, for me, the match of the tournament was Boris Becker's performance against Andre Agassi. He won in four sets after being one set down and 1–4 down in the second set and looking outclassed up to that point. One should also remember he had lost the last eight times he'd played Andre Agassi, so he was at a great psychological disadvantage. It was a classic. Boris, a serve-and-volley exponent, had to do what he does best as well as rallying from the baseline at the highest level. His patience and focus in that match were outstanding.

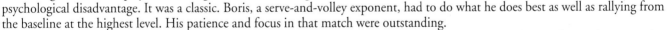

In the other semi-final, between Goran Ivanisevic and Pete Sampras, we had to wonder at the excellence of Goran's serve and the resilience of Pete Sampras.

Not to be outdone, the ladies provided two excellent, hard-fought semi-finals followed by an amazing final when Arantxa Sanchez Vicario won the hearts of the crowd and the true grit of Steffi Graf won the match – as she had done in a similar manner in the 1991 and 1993 finals when she came from behind.

Jana Novotna and Conchita Martinez played their parts in the exciting semi-finals but were overcome by the top two players in the world at the moment.

As Dan Maskell would have said, 'Oh I say!' 1995 was the best Wimbledon I can remember. I am sure this annual will provide a happy memory of The 1995 Championships, as the face of Wimbledon begins to change.

J.A.H. Curry
Chairman
The All England Lawn Tennis & Croquet Club
and the Committee of Management of The Championships

INTRODUCTION

SELDOM had there been a build-up to The Championships when the prospects of the most likely challengers for the men's and ladies' singles titles were so clouded by injuries. The scenario over the previous three weeks, in the countdown to the most important lawn tennis tournament of the year, had been of Andre Agassi, Boris Becker, Steffi Graf and Mary Pierce all needing varying amounts of medical assistance.

The medical bulletins had begun in Paris, where first Agassi, with a pulled hip muscle, and then Pierce, with a shoulder injury to add to the lingering effects of a viral infection, felt obliged to return to the United States for specialist treatment.

Next it was Becker, a three-times former champion, who flew to Germany for help with a calf muscle he strained at the start of the Stella Artois tournament at Queen's Club, which apparently only became a major worry when he was in the semi-finals.

Finally, four days before the start of The Championships, Steffi Graf – whose original intention was to play doubles with Martina Navratilova, in addition to chasing a sixth singles crown – also flew to Germany, worried about a wrist problem, on the day she would otherwise have been paying tribute to the late Fred Perry at his Memorial Service in St Paul's Cathedral.

Add to that the uncertainty about the form of both the defending champions, Pete Sampras and Conchita Martinez, and it all sketched out a catalogue of possibilities, some fascinating, some alarming, depending on just how much notice one took of the reservations being expressed. By now, of course, everyone knows that the worst fears were groundless and that other players, such as Arantxa Sanchez Vicario, were about to earn much greater grass-court credibility than their performances had

Sampras went into Wimbledon '95 aiming to become the only player in modern times, other than Bjorn Borg, to win Wimbledon more than twice in succession. He deserved to be the favourite, albeit with reservations. Even while winning at Queen's Club, which in recent years had not been as reliable a guide to Wimbledon prospects as some imagine, his game lacked that strident authority he had demonstrated on Centre Court in 1993 and 1994.

His clay-court season in Europe had been a disaster. And no one could be absolutely sure how much the American was suffering spiritually from the absence of his coach, Tim Gullikson, with whom he had enjoyed so much success. Of all the memorable moments from the world of tennis in the first half of 1995, one surely stood apart. It was that extraordinarily emotional scene when Sampras broke down and wept during his match against fellow American Jim Courier, at the Australian Open. Gullikson's brain tumour had been diagnosed, and someone in the crowd tried to urge Pete on with a shout of 'Win this one for Gully.'

On the other hand, Sampras knew there would be no better medicine for Gullikson than for him to win Wimbledon again. And there is nowhere in the world which offers Pete Sampras greater inspiration.

The same could also be said of Steffi Graf, and it is strange to think that she did not always have a special affinity with grass courts. The first time she played on the surface, when she was 13, she felt so frustrated by her failure to get her game working that she told her father: 'I never want to go on that surface again.' How things have changed. Two weeks before Wimbledon this year she was asked which was her favourite surface and her favourite tournament. She smiled and replied, 'Still grass . .

THE TO

THE T

THE OFFICIAL CAMERA TO THE CHAMPIONSHIPS, WIMBLEDON 1995. NIKON CAM

FESSIONAL PHOTOGRAPHERS
OL OF
RADE.
AND LENSES. IF YOU
APHS, SO WILL YOU.

andre AGASSI

pete SAMPRAS

1

USA   Age: 25

World Ranking: 1

2

USA   Age: 23

World Ranking: 2

Since overtaking Pete Sampras to become number one on the world rankings in April, Agassi arrived at Wimbledon having not won another tournament. Yet there was no doubting the enormous charisma and appeal of the player who won the US Open in 1994 and the 1995 Australian Open.

On his day and in the right mood, Agassi has the ability to introduce the element of surprise in his game which is the hallmark of a great champion.

While still happier playing from the back of the court than at the net, the way Agassi won Wimbledon in 1992 had reinforced the truth that, on grass, the service return can be just as important as the serve.

After a disastrous clay-court season, during which he lost more matches than he won, Sampras enjoyed the perfect pre-Wimbledon confidence-boost by winning the Stella Artois tournament eight days before The Championships began.

It was a success which convinced the bookmakers to make him the 1–2 odds-on favourite to win the title for a third successive year. Yet despite the almost unanimous backing he received from fellow players when they were asked to nominate the most likely winner, Sampras, by his own standards, had not played well in the first half of the year.

He knew all too well that the serve, on which the success of his whole game is so clearly based, would have to be restored to its traditional Wimbledon potency in order for him to triumph again.

boris BECKER

goran IVANISEVIC

3

Germany	Age: 27
World Ranking: 3	

4

Croatia	Age: 23
World Ranking: 6	

Becker arrived at Wimbledon hoping to celebrate the tenth anniversary of his first triumph in 1985, when, aged 17, he became the youngest men's singles champion. But he was perhaps even more concerned about how an ill-timed injury might thwart his chances.

Just when he had felt he was nicely timing his build-up to the tournament he says means more to him than any other, he strained a calf muscle at Queen's Club and flew home to Germany for almost a week of specialist treatment.

It appeared to be a major blow to the three-times winner, who knew that this might be his last serious opportunity to win another Grand Slam title – but Becker dismissed it as 'just another obstacle to be overcome'.

It was hard to believe that since being runner-up to Sampras in the 1994 final, the left-hander with such a blistering serve had lost to unheralded opponents in the first round of the three intervening Grand Slam tournaments.

Yet that sums up the Croatian's game as well as his personality — magnificent one moment, moody to the point of self-destruction the next.

He is one of those maddeningly gifted players who, once things start to go wrong, especially with his serve, is far more likely to be beaten by his own temperament than by the efforts of his opponent.

michael CHANG

5

USA Age: 23
World Ranking: 5

The most diminutive of the men's seeds but always one of the most energetically determined competitors, Chang was already making his eighth appearance at The Championships.

Having become the youngest winner of the French Open title when he was only 17, in 1989, he has generally been regarded as more of a threat on slow surfaces such as clay than on grass, where the bigger men with extra serving power tend to predominate.

Yet Chang had worked so hard and so effectively to improve his own serve and his general all-court game that fellow players were confidently predicting that he was quite capable of at least matching his best Wimbledon performance, in 1994, when he reached the quarter-finals.

6

Russia Age: 21
World Ranking: 7

The lean, tousle-haired Russian from the Black Sea resort of Sochi has made enormous strides since winning his first tournament in Adelaide in January 1994 and then, a few weeks later, almost beating Pete Sampras at the Australian Open. In 1995 he'd reached the quarter-finals there.

Although brought up on clay, Kafelnikov has a developing all-court game, prompting many to suggest that he could become one of the best players in the world, if not the best. The desire is certainly there

He has already demonstrated his talents impressively on clay, hard and indoor surfaces and in 1994 he also played the principal role when Russia reached the final of the Davis Cup, only to wilt mentally under the pressure and the responsibility. That, however, could easily change with experience.

yevgeny KAFELNIKOV

wayne FERREIRA

7

South Africa   Age: 23

World Ranking: 8

Like so many of his fellow countrymen, Ferreira was a gifted all-round sportsman, representing the Transvaal at soccer, cricket and badminton before confining his sporting talents exclusively to tennis.

Since breaking into the top 20 for the first time in 1992 he has consistently maintained that status, although there was something of a trough in 1994 before everything began to come together again with the support of his wife, Liesl, and new coach, Chris Johnstone.

Although first making his mark in doubles, being number one in the world junior doubles rankings in 1989, he quickly began to excel even more in singles once he joined the men's circuit. His success at Queen's Club in 1992 and his quarter-final appearance at Wimbledon in 1994 make him a more than credible grass-court challenger.

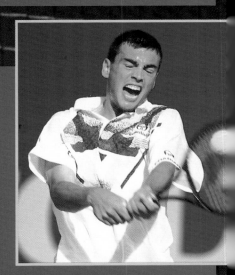

8

Spain   Age: 24

World Ranking: 9

A few days after the draw was done, Bruguera withdrew, citing continuing problems with the knee on which he had undergone arthroscopic surgery in April.

His father and coach, Luis Bruguera, had decided that it was more important for his son, a clay-court specialist, to rest and prepare for later tournaments on clay in Europe, rather than risk his reputation and ranking on grass.

It was a pity for, in 1994, when he returned to Wimbledon after a gap of three years, he not only reached the last 16 but struck 33 winning volleys as he won one of the finest matches of the tournament against Australian serve-and-volleyer, Patrick Rafter.

sergi BRUGUERA

steffi GRAF

1

Germany   Age: 26

World Ranking: 1

Universally recognised as the best player in the world on grass courts, Graf arrived at Wimbledon unbeaten in 26 matches and determined to banish, once and for all, the memory of how she became the first defending champion to be beaten in the first round when she lost to Lori McNeil in 1994.

On her best days, which are numerous, both her serve and forehand have long since been acclaimed as the most important aspects of her match-winning gifts. Equally, that touch of impatience within an obvious perfectionist has still not been finally overcome.

The bookmakers were not being unrealistic in making her odds-on favourite to win for a sixth time in eight years. The biggest danger, it seemed, before The Championships began, was how well her back, weakened by a chronic condition, would stand up to seven matches in 12 days.

arantxa SANCHEZ VICARIO

2

Spain   Age: 23

World Ranking: 2

There was some surprise beforehand when Sanchez was seeded above fellow countrywoman, Conchita Martinez. Though one place below Sanchez in the world rankings, Martinez *was* the defending champion and in 1994 had demonstrated that she could play well on grass.

No one could ever accuse Sanchez of lacking energy or commitment. Her terrier-style retrieving on baselines all round the world has become part of tennis folklore, and many an opponent has been left wondering what on earth more they had to do to finish off points against her.

At Wimbledon, however, Sanchez had never progressed beyond the quarter-finals. Nor, as she would admit, had she really approached the tournament with an abiding, deep-rooted belief that she could do well. The question was, how much had her view changed and her pride been hurt when Martinez beat her to the title as Spain's first winner, 12 months earlier?

conchita MARTINEZ

3

Spain   Age: 23

World Ranking: 3

Amid the obvious emotion of Martina Navratilova's farewell a year earlier, there was still the time and opportunity to admire the performance of the new champion, who beat her in the final.

Martinez had provided more than a gentle hint of her growing understanding of grass courts when she reached the semi-finals in 1993, but it was those staggering backhand passes, not only in the 1994 final but in earlier rounds as well, which marked her out as a player of real substance at Wimbledon.

On the other hand, her form during the autumn and early in 1995 went into serious decline, with her appetite for success, let alone tennis itself, inevitably brought into question. Carlos Kirmayr, the new coach who had been working with her since March, felt he could convince her that she could win Wimbledon again. It was a stern challenge for both of them.

jana NOVOTNA

4

Czech Republic   Age: 26

World Ranking: 5

...tural talent and desire alone, Jana Novotna could – and in 1993 most defi-... should – have won Wimbledon before now. In many ways she is among the ...a dying breed of fully committed serve-and-volleyers in ladies' tennis.

...look so comfortable and effective round the net as this player, brought up ...he extent in the shadow of earlier gifted Czech champions, including her ...Hana Mandlikova and yet . . . too often her skills have been let down by ...actors.

...one needs to remind her of vital matches which slipped away. 'It's not nerves, I ... too hard,' she insists. The truth is probably a bit of both. Novotna remained ...hallenger for Wimbledon '95, though knowing that time was starting to run ...she is to leave a greater legacy than that photograph of her sobbing on the ...ers of HRH the Duchess of Kent.

mary
PIERCE

5

France Age: 20
World Ranking: 4

Pierce, born in Canada, was raised in the United States but then transferred to France when her father was tempted to accept offers of help and opportunities which he did not believe would otherwise be available. She underlined the power in her game and her strength of personality by winning the Australian Open in January.

Yet this would be the first time that this slim, elegant and big-serving competitor would be putting her talent and temperament to the test on the grass courts of The All England Club.

Those working with her had pledged in January that her year had been designed to bring both form and fitness to a peak for the French Open and then Wimbledon – but that was before illness sabotaged the plan. Behind the confident smile, there was an ominous lack of match practice.

kimiko
DATE

6

Japan Age: 24
World Ranking: 6

Like Pierce, though in a less spectacular fashion, Date made her biggest breakthrough at the Australian Open in January when she reached the semi-finals playing solid, reliable, uncomplicated groundstrokes in a typically efficient and resolute Japanese manner.

Her progress over the past couple of years had contributed immensely to the growth of interest and support for tennis in Asia, although at Wimbledon in 1994, when she was also seeded six, she went out in the third round.

Too much of a lightweight game still to be regarded as a potential 1995 champion, the girl who had conquered the art of playing right-handed because her grandmother told her (mistakenly, of course) that no left-hander had succeeded in ladies' tennis, she is capable of upsetting the best-laid plans of others along the way.

idsay DAVENPORT

7

USA Age: 19
World Ranking: 7

In 1994 Davenport arrived at Wimbledon within a couple of days of graduating from high school, and justified American hopes that she could be their next best contender for major titles by reaching the quarter-finals and ruthlessly overwhelming Gabriela Sabatini along the way before losing in three sets to the champion-in-the-making, Martinez.

Yet since then Davenport's progress, like her mobility about the court, had not been as rapid as some had expected and many had hoped, especially in recent months when illness prevented her exploiting her obvious physical strengths – height, weight and reach.

8

Argentina Age: 25
World Ranking: 8

When, in 1990, Sabatini won the US Open title, producing wonderfully instinctive, aggressive, copybook tennis, it was generally expected that the most photographed player in women's tennis would go on to bigger and even better things.

Instead, although her commercial and public popularity have not diminished, her credibility as a consistent world class competitor has clearly slipped, despite her triumph at the Virginia Slims Championships in November 1994 which ended a drought of two-and-a-half years without a tournament title.

The erratic nature of her form is usually most damagingly demonstrated by her serve – and yet one still always believes that there is a wonderful magic ability there somewhere, waiting to break free.

gabriela SABAT

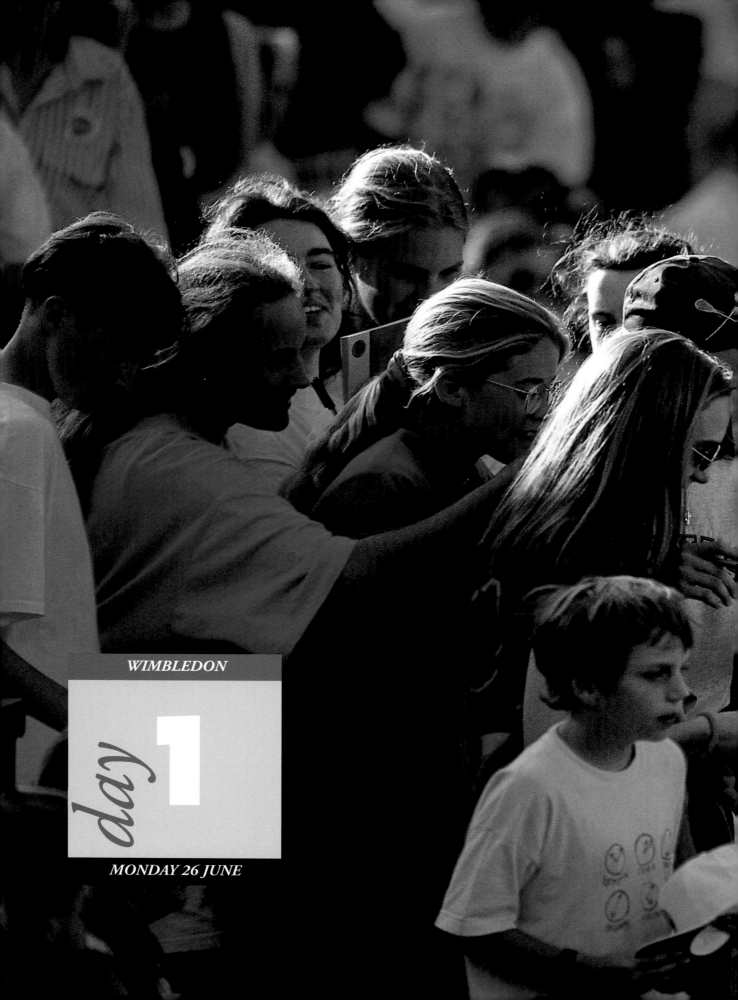

WIMBLEDON

*day*1

MONDAY 26 JUNE

Wimbledon '95 began, as it happily continued for much of the dry fortnight, in a blaze of sunshine, an encouraging amount of British success in the men's singles and much debate over what had been the domestic topic of the summer – new balls.

A few days before The Championships began, the response by John Curry, chairman of The All England Club, when asked to comment, was 'What new balls?' It was an apt response for, despite the furore over the so-called new balls, in fact the only difference was a slight reduction in their pressure, which meant, therefore, they were marginally softer and slower.

Brad Gilbert, coach to Andre Agassi, was so alarmed by reports from London quoting the players as saying the new balls 'were so soft and slow that players would be forced to stay on the baseline' that he immediately arranged for 12 dozen to be despatched to Las Vegas so that the top-seeded former champion, who had returned home from the French Open with a hip injury, could practise with them before flying to England.

More sober thoughts than those initially expressed at Queen's Club came from Pete Sampras. The defending champion dismissed the ballyhoo as 'no big deal' and added, 'Yes, they are softer, which may make it easier for the returner, but it is not going to stop people like myself, Goran Ivanisevic and Boris hitting aces on grass.' It was an astute and prophetic observation, especially as Sampras and Ivanisevic set the balls booming on the first day with 41 aces between them.

Not that Sampras's opening match was entirely convincing. Indeed, he needed the encouragement of two faulty backhands from the entertaining German, Karsten Braasch, before going on to win 7–6, 6–7, 6–4, 6–1 against someone he described with a smile as 'a pain in the ass to play'. Braasch, ranked 120, has never quite been in the mainstream of men's tennis but the bearded, bespectacled left-hander, who is known to enjoy

a pint now and then, and once asked, unsuccessfully, if he could smoke during changeovers at the Australian Open, certainly contributed immensely to the Centre Court launching of The Championships, not least with his slick reactions round the net and his swiftness in swooping on drop shots.

Even though a first-round loser, Jeremy Bates remained a firm favourite with the crowd, as the picture on the previous page illustrates. Karsten Braasch (below) often had to take evasive action from Pete Sampras's power play, opposite.

There was also his intriguing serve, which is unorthodox, to say the least, although like many left-handers, it is supremely effective when swinging away from a right-hander's backhand. Several people watching on television were so convinced that Braasch must be foot-faulting by the way he almost walked into court, arms flailing like a windmill, that they telephoned the referee's office, the press room and the BBC to say so.

Actually, he wasn't. As Sampras said,

It was hard work but worth it for Britain's Tim Henman (below) as he recorded his first singles match win at Wimbledon by beating Kenya's Paul Wakesa. For the more experienced Chris Wilkinson, though, it was smiles all the way after he beat the higher ranked Hendrik Dreekman from Germany.

'It's different – a good serve with a lot of spin making it tough to read. He's a crafty player who volleys well and moves well.' Certainly that was true. Until things changed, once Sampras had broken in the tenth game to take what was clearly a crucial third set, Braasch had not only served more effectively than the recently deposed world number one but also volleyed far better. Confirmation of that came when Sampras said, 'I could have played a lot better', but then added: 'But the important thing on the first day is to get into the tournament and then build up your game round by round from there.'

By contrast with the fight Sampras was given, Ivanisevic, the last player to have beaten the American at Wimbledon, in the 1992 semi-final, found everything sweetness and light, dismissing the Canadian, Sebastien Lareau, 6–2, 6–4, 6–4 with almost immaculate concentration. One can only imagine the relief Ivanisevic must have felt, having lost in the first round of all three intervening Grand Slam tournaments since he had been beaten by Sampras in the 1994 Wimbledon final. It was not a subject on which the Croatian was keen to be drawn. He settled, instead, for two hat-tricks of aces, within his total of 21, one in the second game of the second set, the other in the fourth game of the third.

In what was to be a dreadful year for the lower ranked seeds, the first to fall was Richard Krajicek, when his serve deserted him disastrously in a 7–6, 6–3, 6–3 defeat by the 30-year-old Bryan Shelton, who has excelled on these courts before. One year earlier he had dismissed former champion Michael Stich, in the first round. After Rosmalen, where his serve had also let him down, 12th-seeded Krajicek had stepped up his serving practice sessions but to no avail.

The domestic focal point of attention was, needless to say, the first appearance with 'GB' after his name of Greg Rusedski, who in the preceding two years had won just one match at The All England Club – as a Canadian. The draw had initially placed him opposite the American, Jim Grabb, highly experienced on grass and a more than capable serve-and-volleyer. Just before the match was due to

The familiar sight of Goran Ivanisevic pounding his way to first-round victory against Canada's Sebastien Lareau.

Ross Matheson (above), despite facing a daunting first-round challenge against former semi-finalist, David Wheaton, went closer than any of the others among this quintet of Julie Pullin and Jeremy Bates (left) and the crouching Gary Henderson and the ever-tenacious Danny Sapsford (right) to improving Britain's four out of ten win–loss record on the first day.

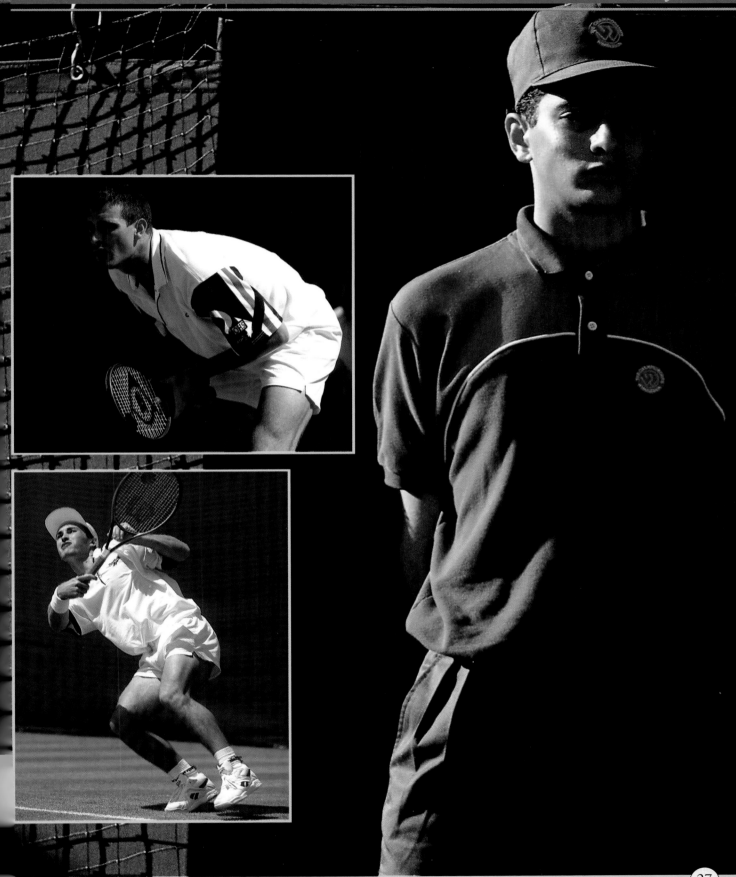

be called, however, Grabb withdrew with an ankle injury and was replaced by Stephane Simian, a lucky loser from the qualifying, who did not pose quite the same threat. Rusedski, with only 20 minutes' notice that he would be facing a changed opponent, did not mind. Having lost in his two previous tournaments as a 'Brit', a win was obviously what he needed and the Court Two crowd, perhaps reserved at first, warmed to the man described by one columnist as Britain's 'grinning white hope', as he hit 12 aces in a 6–3, 6–3, 6–3 victory.

'It helped me a lot,' he said. 'It was just a great feeling to have all those people supporting me. The public have always been good to me here, but nothing like today. If they continue like that, who knows what may happen?'

Four out of ten was to be the mark for British men on the first day, all but three of them – Rusedski, Jeremy Bates and Mark Petchey – having needed wild cards to be involved, but three of them – Tim Henman, Chris Wilkinson and Miles Maclagan – more than justified the chance they had been offered, while Ross Matheson, one point away at one stage from a two sets lead over the 26th-ranked former semi-finalist, David Wheaton, also kept the pulses racing before losing 3–6, 7–5, 7–6, 6–3 to the American.

It was Henman's victory which made the most impact, for his typically efficient 7–6, 6–0, 6–4 defeat of Kenya's Paul Wakesa, who was educated at Millfield, meant that the Oxfordshire player had earned the right to challenge Sampras in the next round. Fully recovered from a serious injury (ironically while he was playing fellow British player Wilkinson in Singapore the previous September), which had left him with three pins in an ankle, Henman took charge after a nervous start for his first victory at The Championships.

Although there was natural concern round Court Two when Henman was broken serving for the crucial first set at

5–4, once he had secured the tie-break 7–3, his game really took off. He broke in the opening game of the second set and then swept through with a series of majestic winners to take it to love in 17 minutes. He lost only five points on the way.

Wilkinson, the most vocal of those who had spoken out against the LTA's decision to embrace Rusedski as one of their own, no doubt felt he had a point to prove as he went out to face Germany's Hendrik Dreekmann and he bravely overcame a heavy cold for a 6–3, 6–4, 7–5 victory, despite being a break down in all three sets. This then gave him the chance for further political, as well as personal satisfaction in round two against Maclagan, the player he had to make way for in Britain's most recent Davis Cup team.

Maclagan also had reason to be pleased rather than surprised as he overcame Renzo Furlan 2–6, 6–2, 7–6, 6–3, for the Italian, who had reached the last eight of the French Open, was still seeking his first win in three visits to SW19.

Yet there was also British disappointment, not least as Jeremy Bates, who had reached the last 16 twice in the three previous years, could never quite pin down the American, Derrick Rostagno, who has always been recognised as a gifted grass-court challenger, and as Petchey crumbled all too rapidly after a first-set tie-break to Mats Wilander, a former world number one back at Wimbledon for the first time since 1989, essentially for fun.

Though most of the women were not taking centre stage until the following day, there was a major upset when Iva Majoli, the teenager the Croatians had been touting as the next Monica Seles, was trounced 6–1, 3–6, 1–6 by Mexico's Angelica Gavaldon, while Gabriela Sabatini kept a well-filled Centre Court happily entertained until 8 p.m. as she beat the 79th-ranked French player, Lea Ghirardi, with her usual mixture of elegant winners – and errors.

'I enjoy the winning now more because before I usually WAS the winner. Now I'm usually the loser.
I never go into a match thinking ahead.
Every match is a big match for me these days.'
Mats Wilander

Wilander (above), on his way to outsmarting Britain's Mark Petchey, had more to enjoy on the first day than Croatian teenager, Iva Majoli, who became the first seed to be beaten.

Boris Becker (previous page) wasted no time in finding his forehand range.

One year after providing the biggest shock of the 1994 championships by defeating defending champion, Steffi Graf in the first round, Lori McNeil (above) was this time a first-round loser herself, against Naoko Sawamatsu. Meanwhile all went smoothly for Mary Pierce (right) when she at last took to the courts at The All England Club for the first time to beat Austria's Sandra Dopfer.

Somehow Ladies' Day, blessed with more wonderfully warm and sunny weather and a record crowd, seemed shorter and tidier than usual. Perhaps the fact that Steffi Graf, Arantxa Sanchez Vicario and Conchita Martinez, the top three seeds, all won in exactly 49 minutes had something to do with that. Such short matches also meant that the presence of five former men's singles champions on court took priority in the public mind, even over the first appearance, at last, at The Championships of Mary Pierce.

Before play began she was the player most wanted to see, while Graf against Martina Hingis, the 14-year-old Swiss prodigy, was the most fascinating match of the day in prospect. At first glance a 6–3, 6–1 defeat for a slim, smiling but modest schoolgirl making her Centre Court as well as her Wimbledon debut against the top-seeded five-times former champion, would seem to have been a worthy effort.

In some ways it was, especially early on when Hingis, one of the last to beat the new rule whereby no one will be accepted for the women's singles in Grand Slam events before they are 16, just as it was before 1975, showed impressive control and strategy from the back of the court. Too often, however, when Graf occasionally lifted her game, she was made to look what she was – a child out of her depth.

On the anniversary of her stunning first-round defeat the previous year, Graf's form was patchy. For every scorching winner there were too many unforced errors, not least when two double faults helped Hingis break back to 2–2 in the first set. The crowd, as one would have expected, was supportive and then increasingly sympathetic to the youngster who said, 'Everything happened so quickly. I didn't have time to react. She was returning so well that I was just hoping she would make mistakes.'

The most significant and alarming moment of the match came in the last game when Graf, who had flown back to Germany for treatment to a wrist injury the previous week, suddenly winced and

then stretched before going into a serv at 30–15 which suggested the back wa worrying her again. 'My back is feelin all right. My wrist is perfect,' she said clearly choosing her words carefully and, indeed, a few hours later came th news that she felt compelled to withdrav from the women's doubles and he much-vaunted new partnership wit Martina Navratilova. More was to be sai about that later.

Martinez said she was 'just happy t be back' on the court where she ha played the most impressive and impor tant match of her life, when winning th title against Navratilova 12 month earlier, after she swept to a 6–1, 6–1 de feat of Sweden's Asa Carlsson in wha was actually a more entertaining matcl than Graf–Hingis. Although one-sided it was not without its bright moments Occasionally Carlsson produced shot which deserved to be winners, but Mar tinez was generally able to respond, espe cially when it came to counter-hitting with something even better.

Sanchez overwhelmed the 90th ranked Katerina Studenikova 6–2, 6– and then declared for the first time i more than just the expected but routin manner that she believed she could wir Wimbledon. 'If the weather stays lik this and I'm playing as consistently as did today, then I must have chances,' sh said, drawing comfort not only from th way Agassi had won the men's title fron the back of the court in 1992 but ever more from the triumph by fellov Spaniard, Martinez, in 1994. It was no just fortuitous that, in addition to he usual coach, Gabriel Urpi, one of her for mer advisers, Australian Mervyn Rose one of the most astute grass-court player of his day, was also around to guide anc encourage her on a surface she had neve before really trusted.

She confessed that maybe in the past believing her prospects to be slim, sh had not prepared as well as she shoul have done. On the other hand, her clain that she now felt ready to vary her tactic between staying back and going to th net still seemed a trifle premature fo

naturally attracted much attention but she was unlucky to draw a confidently aggressive Steffi Graf in the first round.

against Studenikova, she hit winning volleys just twice. Mind you, that was one more than Martinez managed against Carlsson.

Graf, who had taken so long going through her compulsory pre-match stretching exercises that she then had to rush to the court, and only just made it in time for her opening match, was not the only one who exercised a woman's privilege to be late. Pierce kept Austria's Sandra Dopfer waiting alone for four minutes while collecting rackets which had been restrung before making a typically regal entrance to a packed Court 14, where she proceeded to sweep aggressive winners for a 6–1, 6–2 victory in 52 minutes.

It took Pierce a few games to get the feel of what she had always regarded as an alien surface but it was generally a brisk, businesslike performance from the Canadian-born, Florida-based French holder of the Australian Open title, so much so that the girl who did not even pluck up courage to enter Wimbledon until two years earlier, but then dropped out through illness on the morning of her first match in 1993 and for various 'personal' reasons in 1994, regretted not having accepted the challenge earlier.

'I wish that even when I was 14, 15 or 16, when I was playing other tournaments, I had done so but I had this feeling that grass wasn't good for me. I guess it comes with playing matches, maturing and getting experience. Now I think it's OK.' It was a feelgood factor which was not to be sustained.

While Pierce, aged 20, was fully experiencing Wimbledon for the first time, Britain's Jo Durie knew that for her, at 34, and forced to run on what she called 'the knees of a pensioner', this would be her farewell. Now so low in the world rankings that she needed a wild card for this 18th appearance at The Championships, Durie wanted nothing more than to compete well. She certainly did that, often displaying all the athleticism of her youth as she delighted the Court Two crowd by beating Alexia

Dechaume-Balleret from France, 6–2, 7–6.

She was given a standing ovation – by no means her last of the week – and there were tears of joy mingled with relief as she said later, 'This has been my life.' The former British number one said she was now forced to retire, for her specialist had told her that if she had a fourth

Even though many felt he was masquerading as a fugitive from 'The Pirates of Penzance', it did not prevent Andre Agassi's powerful skills shining through (left) as he swept past Australian qualifier, Andrew Painter, while Jo Durie (below) was Britain's heroine for a record second-day crowd of 34,687.

operation on her wonky left knee, she would end up with no knee cap.

On a day when two other British players, Clare Wood and Karen Cross, had already lost, Durie shrugged off having her serve broken to trail 3–4 in the second set by immediately breaking back to love and then took command in the tie-break which she ended with a perfect cross-court volley. Not for the first time, during a grim period for women's tennis in Britain, Durie was the sole domestic first-round survivor.

While Durie prevailed, however, Wimbledon was almost certainly bidding farewell to two of the crowd's favourite foreign visitors, Henri Leconte and Pat Cash. Leconte, the Fernandel of men's tennis and another who has suffered the ravages of injuries, lost 6–3, 6–4, 6–4 to Javier Frana from Argentina and then sadly admitted, 'It's getting more difficult, very difficult. For me, at the age of 32, you just have to realise that some days you can no longer produce the best. You try but you just can't. It's always difficult to stop when you love tennis and when you love the place. For me it hasn't been a job but pleasure, but I think this will be my last Wimbledon.'

Cash's return to the scene of his greatest triumph eight years earlier, when he trounced Ivan Lendl in a one-sided 1987 final, did not even last the distance. After only one set against Dick Norman of Belgium, of whom much more was to be heard later, the veteran Australian, still frustrated over a set point he had missed in an 8–6 tie-break, also felt that his recurring ankle injury would not see him through at least two more sets and retired.

He was not the only former champion to depart prematurely. Michael Stich, the 1991 champion, suffered his second consecutive first-round loss when he was beaten 6–4, 7–6, 6–1 by Jacco Eltingh, in what, on the Dutchman's known grass-court form, had always looked likely to provide an upset. 'He did everything better than me, serve, return, volley,' said Stich, who looked increasingly resigned to defeat from the moment he was broken in the fourth game of the third set.

On the other hand, the three other former champions on duty, Andre Agassi, Stefan Edberg and Boris Becker – though somewhat less impressively than he would have expected or wanted against the Spanish lucky loser, Emilio Alvarez – all advanced. Agassi brushed aside a nervous Australian qualifier, Andrew Painter, with consummate ease and dismissed fears that his recent injury might have dented his longer term prospects by denying him essential hours on the practice courts with a typically mischievous response. 'My feeling is that the more you play on grass, the worse you get' – a comment which was to return to haunt him in the semi-finals.

While Boris Becker had an untroubled first-round win, fellow German and former champion Michael Stich (below) was well beaten by Holland's splendidly effective serve-and-volleyer, Jacco Eltingh.

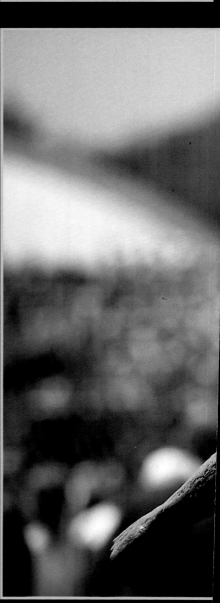

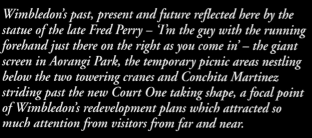

Wimbledon's past, present and future reflected here by the statue of the late Fred Perry – 'I'm the guy with the running forehand just there on the right as you come in' – the giant screen in Aorangi Park, the temporary picnic areas nestling below the two towering cranes and Conchita Martinez striding past the new Court One taking shape, a focal point of Wimbledon's redevelopment plans which attracted so much attention from visitors from far and near.

day **3**

WEDNESDAY 28 JUNE

Chanda Rubin in pensive mood as she contemplates her next move against Patricia Hy-Boulais in what became the longest set played by women at The Championships.

If there had been any doubt about how British fans would respond to Greg Rusedski's arrival, it was swept away on a tide of joyous admiration and emotion as the Centre Court crowd rose wholeheartedly to acclaim him after he had bludgeoned 16th-seeded Guy Forget to second-round defeat with an astonishing display of his ferocious serving.

When, in his first two tournaments after the International Tennis Federation had cleared him to represent Britain (he has a British passport because his mother was born in Dewsbury), Rusedski was beaten in two first-round matches, he said it was just a matter of getting his first serve back into the groove. He certainly did that against the Frenchman, who twice in the previous three years had outserved and outreturned Jeremy Bates

in the fourth round. Rusedski hit 28 aces in a 1–6, 7–6, 7–6, 7–5 victory.

A match which would probably have been assigned to Court 14 or beyond but for Britain's adoption of a man who had been Canada's highest-ranked player, overshadowed even the earlier Centre Court defeat of Mary Pierce by another French player, Nathalie Tauziat, and helped divert some of the attention away from events later in the day when Tim Henman, a born and bred new generation Brit, became the first player to be disqualified in Wimbledon history.

In response to the enormous and prolonged cheering which greeted his victory, Rusedski leapt up, punching the air, before tossing his headband, then a spare shirt and finally a racket into the crowd. 'It's the best feeling – even better than winning my first Tour title,' said Rusedski. 'I'd never been out on Centre Court before and to get a victory there is just a bonus. I'd dreamt of winning on this court. It was very emotional and the crowd had a lot to do with it.'

The tension towards the end, as Rusedski got to within two points of victory at 5–4 and then began his next service game with two double faults, was incredible and came to a climax in the 12th game when he produced a blistering forehand pass to reach his first match point. Forget's response was a brave and biting winning serve, swinging away from the Rusedski forehand. Yet on the next point even a Frenchman who likes playing so much on grass that he regrets that he was not born in England, lost his nerve. He snatched at a backhand volley and it landed beyond the baseline. Forget's first serve as he faced match point a second time was wide of the sideline by a whisker. Rusedski's return of the second serve was by no means one of his best but his fellow left-handed opponent, usually so secure in such situations, mistimed another volley which flew too long.

Rusedski's prospects had not looked bright when he lost the first set in 18 minutes, and he did not begin to settle

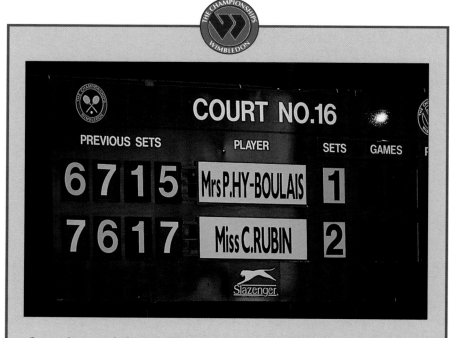

Court 16 is one which more often attracts passing, rather than rapt attention but that was not so on Day Three as Chanda Rubin from the United States and Patricia Hy-Boulais became engaged in a record-breaking encounter. After two tie-breaks, they fought for another 32 games in the final set before Rubin, the 1992 junior girls' singles champion, won 7–6, 6–7, 17–15. The three hour 45 minute match produced the longest set ever played by women at Wimbledon; the total number of games – 58 – surpassed the record which had been set by A. Weivers of France and O. Anderson of the United States, in 1948.

until he had changed his shoes when 0–5. From then on, though, it was a match in which the serve was often paramount and, as Forget said, it was always going to be a matter of 'one or two points here and there. The match turned on one I gave to him on match point, one in the tie-break of the second set and the net cord he played in the third-set tie-break.'

He was right. Forget led 5–2 in the second-set tie-break, but when serving at 5–4 was caught by one of a growing number of perfectly chipped, low paced returns. Then, with the third-set tie-break going with serve, Rusedski broke for 5–3 with a clipped backhand service return which hit the tape and dribbled over on the Frenchman's side. The ace with which he completed that tie-break was 134 mph, Rusedski's fastest of the match – and the fastest recorded (on Centre Court) by anyone during the fortnight.

Over on Court One, Henman was put under close scrutiny by Pete Sampras. 'He reminds me a little bit of Jeremy Bates. He does everything well but needs to develop a weapon,' said the

American after a much sharper performance than in his previous match for a 6–2, 6–3, 7–6 victory in which Henman played almost as well as he was allowed to but suffered heavily from ten double faults. By contrast it was not until midway through the second set that Henman

Greg Rusedski yells with leaping delight at the end of his memorable defeat of 16th-seeded Frenchman, Guy Forget, who, while waiting to congratulate the victor, contemplates the net cord which cost him a crucial mini-break in the third-set tie-break.

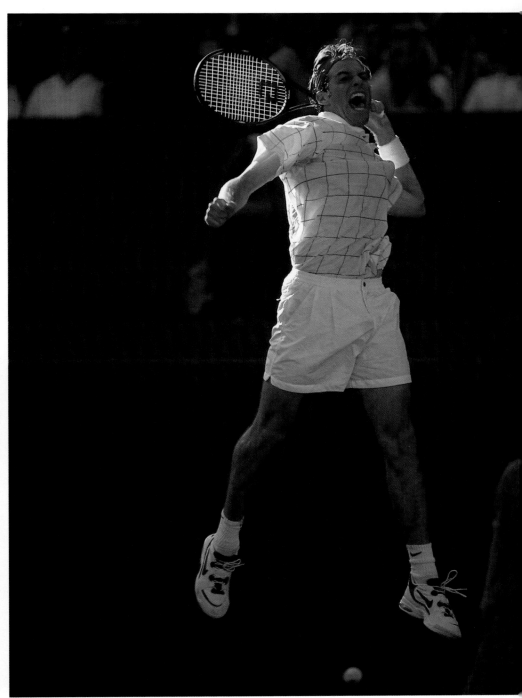

'It's the best feeling – even better than winning my first Tour title. I'd never been out on Centre Court before and to get a victory there was just a bonus. I'd dreamt of winning on this court. It was very emotional and the crowd had a lot to do with it.'
Greg Rusedski

took his first point, apart from double faults, off the Sampras serve.

In normal circumstances Henman could have looked back on that match and the day with a good deal of satisfaction and encouragement. At 9.18 p.m., before a still well-filled crowd on Court 14, however, the day turned into a disaster when he accidentally injured a ball girl after losing a crucial point in the fourth-set tie-break and for that, the rules state unequivocally, there is only one outcome – the player (or in the case of doubles, the player and his partner, Jeremy Bates) must be defaulted.

The incident happened when Henman and Bates were leading Sweden's Henrik Holm and the American, Jeff Tarango, 7–6, 2–6, 6–3 and the fourth set had just gone into a tie-break. Henman was broken on both his serves for the British pair to go 1–2 down, the second of them on a lucky net cord by Tarango, who did not help matters by telling the umpire what he thought about it (and was, of course, to feature in a much more notorious controversy a few days later).

Henman, close to tears, admitted he had been angry at the way he lost a crucial point. 'I went to hit the ball to the other end (where it then needed to go anyway). I admit I hit it hard but I'd

looked to see if the linespeople were out of the way first. Then, just as I threw the ball up to hit it, the ball girl ran across the net and it hit her on the side of the head. If I hadn't hit her with the ball, it wouldn't even have been a code violation, but I know I must accept responsibility for my actions,' said Henman, who increased, rather than reduced support for him by the way he handled himself in the situation.

Meanwhile there was no need for any apology from Goran Ivanisevic to those who prefer baseline rallies to serve-and-volley cannons, after he struck 28 aces in

Pete Sampras (below) congratulates Tim Henman on a good effort in the second round but there was only frustration (right) and tension (far right) for Mary Pierce, as she was beaten by a jubilant fellow French player, Nathalie Tauziat (bottom right).

a 6–4, 6–2, 7–6 win over Jonathan Stark, the American chosen by Martina Navratilova for the mixed doubles, where she hoped to compensate, at least in part, for the way Steffi Graf had left her without a partner for the women's doubles.

The former world champion was clearly not well pleased. 'At just about every Grand Slam she's got something wrong with her body. That's why I wanted to play mixed as well because I thought Steffi might pull out. It's not my body, but if it were me I would at least try to play a match or two and see how it goes. But what could I do?' she continued. 'Twist her arm and say, "You've got to play me with me because I want you to." No, of course not. What good would that do? I took it like a man – on the chin!'

The defeat of Pierce, on a day when Arantxa Sanchez Vicario, Conchita Martinez and Gabriela Sabatini all advanced in straight sets – but not always in straightforward fashion – was not a major surprise to those who realised Tauziat's extra experience on grass. Also, just as not everyone in British tennis welcomed Rusedski with open arms, so there remain mixed feelings among some other French players about the way the imported Pierce has usurped them.

As Pierce's coach, Nick Bollettieri said: 'Tauziat's body language showed it was war. She came to do battle; Mary was gun-shy.'

Tauziat, who won 6–4, 3–6, 6–1, attacked at every opportunity and Pierce had no answer. 'When she first arrived in France we were all against her but now she plays for us she's nice to us.' Yet that did not stop her adding, 'But every chance I get to beat her, I take it.'

Finally, Chris Wilkinson could have been forgiven a rueful smile after he not only beat but trounced Miles Maclagan, the player who, though much lower ranked, had been preferred to him in the well-beaten British Davis Cup team against the Slovak Republic in April. It was a victory which made the Southampton player the first British competitor to reach the third round in three successive years since Mark Cox in 1970.

Arantxa Sanchez Vicario moved serenely into the third round against Japan's Mana Endo, but the 'Way Out' sign was the one Miles Maclagan was forced to follow when he was outplayed by fellow Briton, Chris Wilkinson.

WIMBLEDON

day **4**

THURSDAY 29 JUNE

Stefan Edberg, twice the champion, found himself dwarfed in more ways than one in the second round by Belgium's 6ft 8in qualifier, Dick Norman, while Petr Korda (right) was ecstatic, after several months of struggle, about his surprise defeat of fifth-seeded Michael Chang.

Four more seeds were knocked out of the men's singles on Day Four and that, after one, Sergi Bruguera, had not even made it to the starting line, meant that only seven, the lowest total in the Open era, had survived until the round of the 32. Yet disappointing though it obviously was for those who had been beaten, not least former champion Stefan Edberg and his large army of loyal supporters, it was equally significant that none among those given the best chance of winning the title had so far seriously faltered.

Edberg, opening the proceedings on Court 14, was upset 6–3, 6–4, 6–4 by Dick Norman, a 6ft 8in giant of a man with a serve to match who, despite his name, is a Belgian, barely recognised in his own country, let alone at Wimbledon, until he came back into the event

after being beaten in the qualifying a Roehampton as the fourth among six lucky losers.

Journalist Patrick Haumont of *L Libre Belgique* confided: 'The only Norman they know of in Belgium is Greg Norman.' Dick was ranked only seventh within Belgium and had never won any kind of Belgian title or been included in a Davis Cup squad.

Norman, who had profited from the first-round retirement of another former Wimbledon winner, Pat Cash, had spent much of the two previous years recovering from serious cartilage injuries and this was the first Grand Slam tournament of his career. 'If I continue to serve like I did today I can take a lot of good players out of the tournament,' he said, before adding what was also all too true

that he knew 'Stefan didn't play so well.' As has so often happened in the last couple of years, when Edberg's serve lets him down, the rest of his game becomes a problem too. He was just unable to string enough good points together. Ironically, on a day when one of the last representatives of grass-court elegance in men's tennis was losing, his former coach Tony Pickard's new pupil, Petr Korda from the Czech Republic, upset fifth-seeded Michael Chang 6–4, 6–4, 6–4. After a difficult couple of years which had seen his ranking drop considerably from the top ten to the mid-50s, Korda suddenly found the control which had been missing from his aggression.

The crucial game came when Korda was serving for the second set. He squandered five set points, more than one on double faults, but he eventually held and a break in the ninth game of the third set ended the American's defiance.

Jim Courier, without a Grand Slam win since the Australian Open in 1993, was also in need of renewed success at Wimbledon but that hope vanished when he was handsomely beaten by the all-action Frenchman, Cedric Pioline, also 6–4, 6–4, 6–4. Pioline rained down big serves but also came up with more than enough passes and appetising touch shots round the net to beat the 11th seed, who could also have wished for rather better luck than he experienced in the third set.

A net cord which gave Pioline a second match point was frustrating enough. Having escaped that by breaking his opponent for the first time, however, worse followed. Most of the crowd thought that the serve which earned Pioline a fourth match point had clipped the net but it was not called. It was all over.

Three minutes later, on the adjacent Court Three, Andrei Medvedev became the third men's seed of the afternoon – and certainly the most unexpected – to fall when he simply could not find even the enthusiasm, let alone the strategy, to thwart the American, Jeff Tarango, who advanced 6–4, 6–3, 4–6, 6–2.

No such problems for top-seeded Andre Agassi. On a day when the still-soaring temperatures on Centre Court reached 102 degrees F, he trounced Patrick McEnroe 6–1, 6–1, 6–3 and then said: 'I'm seeing the ball really clean, picking it up quick and I'm very confident.' McEnroe's brother, John, was commentating on the match for American viewers and possibly pondering also on how much things have changed since his heyday at Wimbledon. He'd escaped with little more than some stern tut-tutting for his 'pits of the world' outburst, among others. On this particular day Tim Henman heard he had been fined £1,950 for being disqualified – correctly, but some felt for rashly impetuous rather than wilful behaviour in the men's doubles the night before.

Patrick McEnroe was struggling from the moment Agassi broke in the third game. It was a considerable tour de force from the 1992 champion, still not yet fully tested. 'If you're going to get beat, you might as well get beat badly by the best,' said McEnroe philosophically. 'The way he's playing, he obviously has a good chance of winning it again, but he's going to come up with a few guys who can give him more problems than I could,' he added. How true that was to be.

Despite having a tough time serving out for the first set and losing his way in the second when the volleying skills of Swedish doubles specialist, Jan Apell came to the fore, Boris Becker also moved steadfastly enough into round three with a 6–3, 3–6, 6–1, 6–2 victory. Often sitting at changeovers with a towel draped over his head to protect himself from the scorching sun, Becker emphatically lifted his game in the third and fourth sets in a way which justified his growing optimism.

On the women's front, Steffi Graf survived a second-set fright, largely of her own making, before beating South African, Amanda Coetzer, 6–3, 7–5 and she admitted that there were times when her mind was focusing more on her troublesome back than the match. 'Although it didn't affect me or give me any pain, sometimes I was waiting for something to happen for you can never tell when it is going to happen.'

What had looked like being a routine contest for Graf came alive when, on her first match point, she made no attempt

On a day when temperatures soared beyond 100 degrees F on Centre Court, Patrick McEnroe (left) took a roasting from Andre Agassi and Andrei Medvedev (below) also surprisingly wilted in the sun against Jeff Tarango.

to cut off a defensive return thinking it would go into the net. While she was preparing to offer Coetzer a victory, the shot flew past her as a winner and that set off a stream of winners for the South African as she rallied from 2–5 to 5–5.

The only women's casualty among the seeds on this day was Helena Sukova. No longer the serve-and-volley force of former years, the Czech Republic player surprisingly went down to Japan's Yone Kamio, 4–6, 6–4, 6–4.

A ball boy, well protected against the heat, poised and ready to assist Steffi Graf and Amanda Coetzer.

Michael Chang (below) found Petr
Korda's tennis, like the weather, too hot
for him on this occasion, while Jonas
Bjorkman (bottom left) was outclassed by
Wayne Ferreira (top right). Tim Henman
said sorry with flowers to Caroline Hall,
the ball girl he had accidentally struck
the night before. Hitting that ball in
anger made him the first player in
Wimbledon history to be disqualified.

Jana Novotna proved too durable for Jo Durie.

It was the time for unashamed sentiment on Court One, where another standing ovation was the crowd's tribute to Jo Durie after her singles career at Wimbledon came to an end with a 6–2, 6–2 defeat by Jana Novotna in 70 minutes.

As the ovation continued, Durie, who had never gone beyond the quarter-finals but at least included a 1984 fourth-round win over Steffi Graf in her Wimbledon record, trotted to the far side of the court to embrace Alan Jones, her coach for all of her 18 years in professional tennis. It was not until later, when she realised they were assessing the match in their customary fashion, that the significance of retirement fully dawned. 'It was crazy,' she giggled. 'That was my last match and yet there we were analysing it with me thinking about what I would need to work on for next week. Then I remembered . . . Oops, that's it.'

On the day when Greg Rusedski (overleaf) waved the Union Jack flag for Britain by reaching the fourth round, others wilted in the 110 degree F heat, with a clearly distressed Shirli-Ann Siddall having to be taken off court on a stretcher after collapsing from heat exhaustion during her mixed doubles with Danny Sapsford. Meanwhile Jared Palmer (below left) and Pete Sampras had ball boys and girls to help keep them cool under the umbrellas at changeovers.

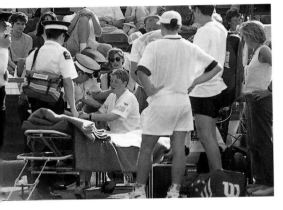

The patriotic celebrations which Greg Rusedski had inspired on the Centre Court two days earlier were continued even more spectacularly and excitely on Court One as Britain's new tennis hero aced his way into the last 16 with a 6–7, 6–4, 6–4, 7–6 victory over Olivier Delaitre. As the last of his 36 aces, a personal record, flew past the racket of the third Frenchman in succession to lose to Britain's adopted son from French-speaking Quebec, Rusedski not only went through his leaping, air-punching routine again but then unfurled the Union Jack flag he had worn as a headband for most of the two hour 29 minute match and held it proudly aloft to all four sides of the court.

No racket followed this time, as after he had beaten Guy Forget, but Rusedski's joy at the way he had again fought back from losing the first set, and the reception he received, knew few bounds. 'It's just been phenomenal the way the crowd has reacted to me. I've never had such support in my life,' said the left-hander, as he was then able to contemplate another Centre Court appearance, this time against Pete Sampras, and the chance to become the first British quarter-finalist since Roger Taylor went on to become a semi-finalist in 1973.

On a day when the temperature rose even higher, to 110 degrees F, the highest of the fortnight (though slightly less than the 112 degrees F record set a year earlier), Rusedski could hardly have made a more encouraging start, with two second-serve aces in the first game, which he completed with a wonderful cross-court backhand. Yet after the only break point of the first set had eluded him in the sixth game, it looked as if Delaitre's steadier returns and sharper volleys might be enough to tame a swashbuckling serve. Too often Rusedski did not appear to have enough other talents in his game. Having saved the first set points against him with the bravest of aces, at 5–6 in the tie-break, he then played two weak points to fall behind. Once he moved ahead in the second,

however, with an early service break, the whole momentum and shape of the match changed.

Delaitre began making unforced volleying errors. Double faults also crept in with increasing, undermining regularity, not least when he committed one of each such blunders to gift Rusedski a service break for 3–2 in the third. And although the Frenchman led 3–0 in the fourth set, more volleying errors helped Rusedski draw level and then dominate the match-winning tie-break.

So Rusedski, who by then had delivered 77 aces in three matches, advanced – but without the companionship of his arch-critic, Chris Wilkinson, who, despite fighting grittily for most of his 5–7, 6–4, 7–6, 6–4 defeat by Californian Michael Joyce, ranked above him, could and should have won. Wilkinson led 3–0 with two points for 4–0 in the second set and held a point for the third set at 6–5 but, just when he needed them most, his returns of a far from over-menacing Joyce serve let him down.

Elsewhere, in the bottom half of the draw, Sampras recovered capably after an uncertain start to beat Jared Palmer in four sets, while Goran Ivanisevic, beginning to sense more than ever that perhaps this might be his year, was devastatingly powerful and concentrated as he swamped Arnaud Boetsch, a Frenchman who has said he would like to become Swiss, 6–4, 6–4, 6–4. 'It's a joke, I was playing a giant. It's like he's not playing the same game,' he said, as one after another of the 22 aces whistled past him. Boetsch, who more than once acknowledged the almost terrifying pace and power in his opponent's play, said: 'You're under such pressure that he only has to play one good game to break you in each set and it's over.' Ivanisevic had done just that.

Todd Martin, whose form had slipped like his ranking for much of the year, produced one of his sharpest performances for some time in recovering from two sets to one down to beat the stylish Derrick Rostagno in five sets, while

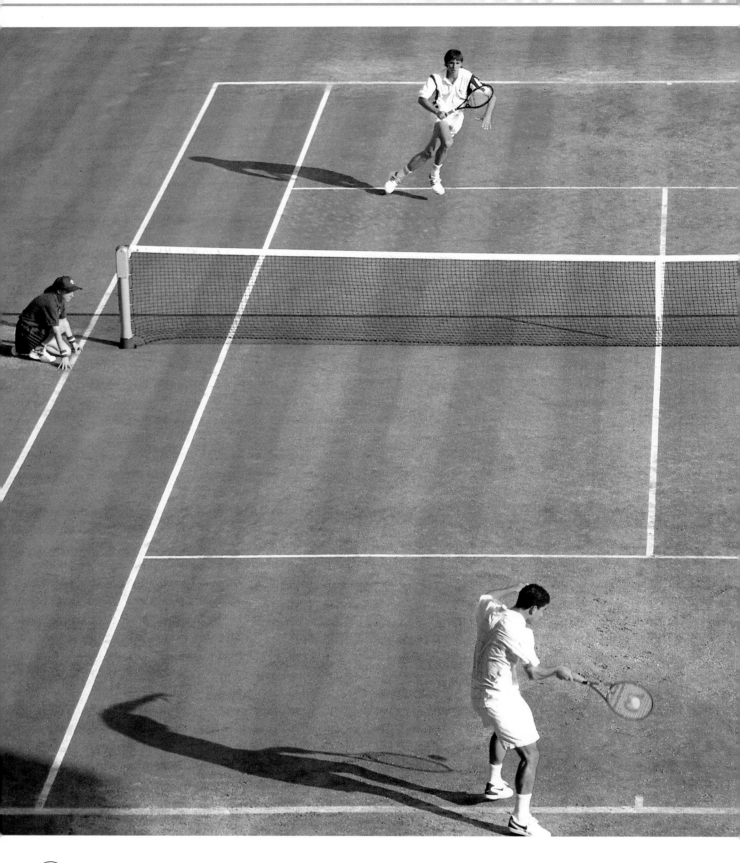

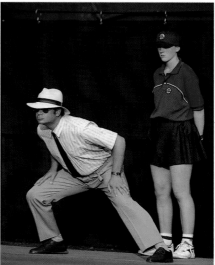

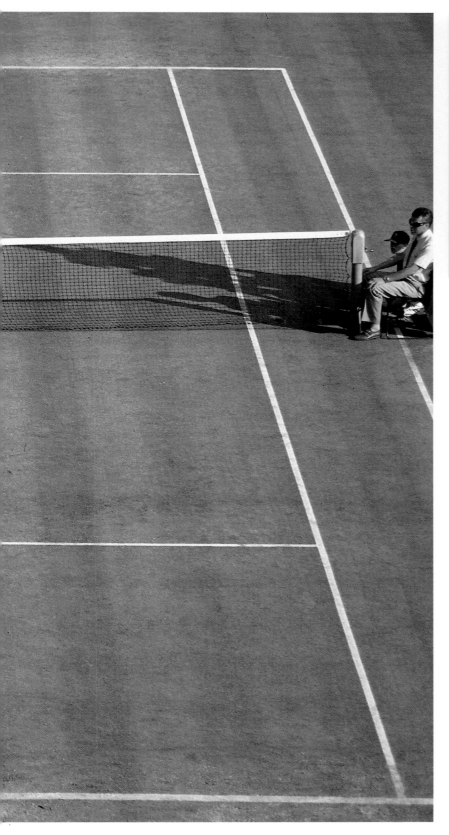

Greg Rusedski (overleaf) played with boundless energy to beat Olivier Delaitre on Court One, while Pete Sampras and Jared Palmer kept match officials on the alert by frequently hitting close to the lines.

'In 1992 I served 206 aces during the two weeks but still only finished second. I'd rather just hit one if it meant winning the tournament.'

Goran Ivanisevic after 22 aces, including one of 129 mph on a second serve, as he overwhelmed Arnaud Boetsch

The stylish Yayuk Basuki (above) kept her nerve despite losing the first set as she floored Nathalie Tauziat (left).

in a five-set
, but
d the
at fellow

Shuzo Matsuoka became the first Japanese player since Jiro Yamagashi in 1934 to reach the last 16 when he beat Javier Frana, also from two sets to one down, with the Argentinian twice complaining about the noisily exuberant support his opponent was receiving from many of his fellow countrymen in the Court 13 crowd. Yevgeny Kafelnikov, the sixth seed, beat fellow Russian Alexander Volkov in three sets, a match which failed to stir the Centre Court crowd but had the merit of being quick enough for Martina Navratilova then to take to the stage she knows and loves so well, at the start of her mixed doubles campaign.

The sun may have been fading when the holder of more singles titles than anyone launched her bid for the two extra doubles titles she knew she still needed to equal Billie Jean King's overall record, but she entered the scene to a standing ovation and a match which overshadowed the women's singles third-round clashes earlier in the day.

In these, one more seed fell. Naoko Sawamatsu, a surprise first-round winner over Lori McNeil, looked drained of energy after recovering from a set down in both her previous matches, as she lost 6–1, 7–6 to Holland's Petra Kamstra, while Yayuk Basuki put paid to any further advancement for Nathalie Tauziat after her defeat of Mary Pierce. Otherwise it was mostly plain sailing for Arantxa Sanchez Vicario (as she brought the Wimbledon singles career of former runner-up, Zina Garrison-Jackson, to a close by avenging defeat in the same event a year earlier), Conchita Martinez and Anke Huber.

It was not so easy for Gabriela Sabatini. The Argentinian, who still hates to be reminded of how she missed five match points against Mary Joe Fernandez

in the quarter-finals of the French Open in 1993, when a 6–1, 5–1 lead was transformed into a 1–6, 7–6, 10–8 defeat – and then to her dismay 'achieved' something similar against Kimiko Date at the Lipton in March '95, began by losing the first five games to Belgium's Nancy Feber. 'I just wanted to make it a little more exciting,' she explained when, less than an hour later, she had won 7–5, 6–1.

As for Navratilova, who was apparently letting it be known to friends that perhaps she had retired from singles too soon after all, she and Jonathan Stark, an accomplished doubles player in his own right, beat fellow Americans, Matt Lucena and Tami Whitlinger-Jones 6–4, 7–6. It was far from a great match but the crowd enjoyed it just the same.

Arantxa Sanchez Vicario (left) was more than content with the many winners she produced against Zina Garrison-Jackson (top) on a day when spectators basked in the sun and St John's Ambulance staff treated dozens of fainting cases.

Some queued, not only overnight but from as early as the previous morning for the now traditional 'people's day' on middle Saturday, which was to produce one of the most extraordinary incidents in the history of The Championships. Tournament referee, Alan Mills (above), spent much of the week-end sorting out the events on Court 13.

The overnight queues for 'people's day' on middle Saturday were the longest most people could remember and the events which unfolded were quite the most remarkable in Wimbledon history.

Hitherto, probably, not too many people outside the immediate tennis fraternity knew a great deal about 26-year-old Jeff Tarango from Manhattan Beach, California, other than that he was one of a bunch of pretty good middle-range Americans who always seemed to be around, without making it to the final stages of too many events.

Indeed, the record book showed that until Wimbledon '95, where he had upset 15th-seeded Andrei Medvedev to reach the third round, Tarango, a left-hander, had never previously won even one match in six visits to The Champi-

onships. Yet thanks to an explosion of temper on Court 13, and then a chaotic press conference in which his wife, Benedicte, dramatically intervened, the name Jeff Tarango will become deeply engraved in Wimbledon legend.

What basically happened was that Tarango, who lists philosophy and creative writing among his interests, was trailing Germany's Alexander Mronz 7–6, 2–1 on Court 13 when he disputed a line-call. As the crowd started to jeer, he told them to 'shut up' and was promptly given a code violation by French umpire, Bruno Rebeuh – who, it transpired later, was not his favourite match official.

Rebeuh, though one of the most experienced and respected umpires in the game, a full-time professional who

Jeff Tarango became involved in a fierce row with French umpire, Bruno Rebeuh (below) and, despite the intervention of supervisor, Stefan Fransson (left), refused to play on and defaulted himself by stalking off court.

Dick Norman became the first lucky loser, since such records began, to reach the last 16 when he beat Todd Woodbridge.

three weeks earlier had umpired the men's singles final at the French Open for a seventh consecutive year, did not help matters in this instance by announcing, in the pressure of the moment, that the offence had been 'an audible obscenity'. This was later changed to 'verbal abuse'.

Even so, there was no excuse for what followed. Tarango has never been bashful about expressing his feelings and has all too frequently found himself on the wrong side of the disciplinary code – as in Tokyo, in October 1994, when, after losing his serve in the third set of a defeat by Michael Chang, he dropped his shorts to the crowd. 'I thought people were concerned about tennis being entertaining. There has to be some fun and humour' was his explanation.

This time, instead of dropping his shorts he simply laid bare his obsession that almost the whole of the tennis world, and especially umpire Rebeuh, seemed to be against him. When the supervisor, Sweden's Stefan Fransson, arrived on court and refused to rescind the code violation, Tarango yelled in Rebeuh's direction: 'You are the most corrupt official in the game.' As the umpire then announced a point penalty against him, giving Mronz the game, Tarango lifted his arms in the air and shouted: 'That's it, I'm not playing – no way.' He hurled the two balls he had been holding to the ground, collected his spare rackets and stalked off court to jeers and boos.

Mronz, the winner by default, said, 'I've never seen anything like that before' to which, with hindsight, the reply could have been 'You ain't seen nothing yet.' In the press conference which followed, Tarango went into great detail about problems he felt he had unfairly experienced in matches umpired by Mr Rebeuh over several years. And when his French wife suddenly appeared in the room, to admit that she had gone up to Bruno Rebeuh after the match and slapped him 'because if Jeff slapped him he's out of the Tour so I do it because I

think somebody should do it,' he chipped in with 'I'm glad you did that.'

Tarango went on to make serious allegations about the umpire which also implicated other players, specifically Olympic gold medal winner, Marc Rosset, although two days later, after many hours of anguished talking with tournament referee, Alan Mills, chief supervisor, Ken Farrar, and advisors of his own, he totally vindicated the Swiss player of such charges and apologised for causing him embarrassment.

It was a cause célèbre which – partly because of the possibilities for legal action – could not possibly be concluded at Wimbledon. Tarango, who announced he would appeal, was fined £10,000 (a record at The Championships) for his on-court offences, but the more serious matter of what he said and alleged later was left in the hands of Grand Slam administrator Bill Babcock, who merely said that a full investigation would be held and that it might take some time.

Meanwhile a tournament was still being played. Away from those extra-curricular activities, Andre Agassi and Boris Becker both reinforced their threat to Pete Sampras's title, and even Steffi Graf was smiling again as her back and her form returned to shipshape fashion. And the spectacular and thankfully rare glimpse of the squalid side of professional tennis was countered to some extent by the fairytale progress of 6ft 8in Belgian, Dick Norman.

Having already beaten two former singles champions – Pat Cash (through retirement) and Stefan Edberg – Norman now ousted doubles champion, Todd Woodbridge, 6–4, 6–4, 3–6, 6–3, for the right to challenge Boris Becker. 'Jesus . . . another champion,' said the first lucky loser from the qualifying to reach the last 16 that even Wimbledon librarian, Alan Little, could recall – and certainly since such records began in 1986 – as he was given the news of Becker's 2–6, 6–2, 6–2, 6–4 defeat of Holland's Jan Siemerink.

Becker, playing on the Centre Court

for the first time this year, returned far better than he served, at least until the final set when everything in his game was flowing splendidly. His backhand groundstrokes were consistently impressive, and had he taken one of the five break points he'd held in a fascinating first game of the match, which lasted 14 minutes, the whole exercise might have been much more straightforward.

Despite dropping the first set Becker mostly looked confident – perhaps sometimes too confident. For example, on the third break point of that first game, instead of choosing a simple pass, he went for an unduly extravagant lob and missed his target.

For stunning returns, however, there were none to beat the timing, quality and accuracy of those flowing from Agassi's racket as, tested for the first time, the 1992 champion beat fellow American David Wheaton 6–2, 3–6, 6–4, 6–2. Other aspects of Agassi's game were not so reliable, though, and he was briefly in trouble when broken to trail 3–4 in the third set. But from then on the generators were set at full power.

Wheaton, suffering from a leg injury and knowing all too well that the now traditional Wimbledon wave on middle Saturday was not really for his benefit, was allowed only two more games.

Mats Wilander's fun came to an end when, despite leading 4–1 in the first-set tie-break, he could not cope quite well enough with the serve-and-volley strengths of Jacco Eltingh, one of nine

Andre Agassi's tennis sparkled as brightly as his ear-ring once he moved into his stride against fellow American, David Wheaton, on Centre Court.

No amount of pleading from David Wheaton (below) prompted the linesman to change his mind over this call as he lost to Andre Agassi. Jacco Eltingh, meanwhile, enjoyed the afternoon on Court One, where he beat Mats Wilander, rather more than Mark Woodforde (right) who was already on the brink of defeat in five sets before slipping and straining his groin in the last game, needing treatment and reassurance from Danish trainer, Per Bastholt.

The end of the road for Lindsay Davenport against Mary Joe Fernandez but (right) Jana Novotna's fighting spirit wore down Judith Wiesner.

unseeded survivors to the last 16, who probably fancied his chances of moving into the quarter-finals at the expense of Wayne Ferreira. The South African had gone perilously close to becoming the second player of the day to be thrown out of the men's singles before he finally squeezed past Australian Mark Woodforde on Court One.

Ferreira was given a code violation for racket abuse after losing the fourth-set tie-break. Then, in the next game, with Woodforde about to start, a side linesman walked to the middle and reported the seventh seed for allegedly using an obscenity. Umpire Richard Kaufmann accepted Ferreira's explanation that the word he used in Afrikaans was harmless compared to the English word it sounded like, but the delay clearly distracted Woodforde, who lost the game and never recovered. The heavy fall he took, straining his groin in the last game, was all Woodforde needed. Ferreira won 6–1, 1–6, 6–4, 6–7, 6–2.

In the women's singles, Graf served magnificently as she brushed aside Holland's Kristie Boogert, by no means an automatic pushover on grass, 6–1, 6–0 in 43 minutes. 'One of those days when everything worked well,' beamed Graf. 'I hadn't expected it to be like that, but it was nice that it happened.'

Graf's next opponent would be Ines Gorrochategui, who progressed from a set down and 3–3 in the second to beat the mercurial Natasha Zvereva 2–6, 6–4, 6–4, while on Centre Court Austria's Judith Wiesner did not do quite enough to send alarm bells ringing in Jana Novotna's mind. The Czech Republic player got by, though none too confidently, 7–5, 6–4.

Finally, two days after Court One bade a sentimental farewell to Jo Durie, it was the turn of those on Centre Court to give her an even more resounding send-off. Her Wimbledon career ended at 9.25 p.m. as she and Jeremy Bates, the 1987 mixed doubles champions, went down 6–3, 5–7, 9–11 in the second round to Australians Andrew Florent and Catherine Barclay.

Durie, who hugged Bates at the end and left with a few waves, amid enormous cheers, said: 'I couldn't think of a better way to go.'

WIMBLEDON

day **7**

MONDAY 3 JULY

The start of the second week is generally regarded as the most significant staging post in The Championships. With a full round of last 16 matches in both the men's and women's singles, it usually provides a better guide than anything which has gone before to those players with the best chance of carrying off the titles.

So it proved again this year, when one could recall the second Monday as the day when the eventual champions, although not alone in doing so, first indicated that they were clearly running into their best form at the right time.

Pete Sampras, for instance, easily outclassed Greg Rusedski on the day the latter had been nominated to make his Davis Cup debut for Britain, beating him 6–4, 6–3, 7–5. More than one correspondent pointed out how peculiarly British it was for the crowd to rise and acclaim their new hero even though he had just lost the match on a double fault.

Yet although the reality of the situation was that, well though he fought, Rusedski could never fully counter the superior skills, especially off the ground, of his gifted opponent, this personable young man had done enough in his four matches to suggest that he could provide an inspirational torch for British youngsters to follow.

On a day when the temperatures were thankfully well down from the scorching heat of the first week – which had led to Britain's Shirli-Ann Siddall collapsing with heat exhaustion in her mixed doubles match with Danny Sapsford – Sampras, Andre Agassi and Boris Becker all scored heavily with their returns, while Steffi Graf continued her effortless progress by reaching the quarter-finals for the eighth time.

Even so, it was the Rusedski–Sampras clash which had most captured the public imagination. Some had queued since early on Saturday in the hope that perhaps a left-hander with Yorkshire ancestry could emulate the achievement of another Yorkshire left-hander, Sheffield's Roger Taylor, in knocking out a defending champion (Rod Laver, in 1970). It

was, of course, asking too much.

Sampras, as he indicated later, knew the match would be his if he could return some of Rusedski's biggest serves because he felt the rest of his opponent's game, especially his return, was 'pretty average'. Rusedski, who had to survive a break point as early as the first game, knew he had to serve exceptionally well from start to finish, and return with outstanding consistency. Even then he would have to hope that the best grass-court player in the world might make a number of uncharacteristic unforced errors.

In the event none of Rusedski's three wishes was fulfilled, though he was a trifle unfortunate in the way Sampras broke his serve for the first time in the seventh game. At deuce, there was an unusual delay between Rusedski's first and second serves as the ball girl played hide and seek with a ball which disappeared under the canvas at the side of the court. When they resumed, Rusedski not only double-faulted but was passed by another among a whole series of immaculate backhands which flowed from the American's racket on the next point.

Naturally most of his new army of British fans were sorry to see Rusedski depart – although perhaps not the Wimbledon groundstaff. Unlike the vast majority of male players today, Rusedski does not jump into his serve but (like another left-hander, John McEnroe), scrapes his left toe into the baseline as he serves, creating a little trench that deepens the longer the match goes on. What with that, and the divots he seemed to take out of the turf because of the sheer power and pace of his serves, there always seemed to be three or four members of head groundsman Eddie Seaward's team standing by between every other changeover to make quick repairs.

In the end it was 6–4, 6–3, 7–5 to Sampras. The American, reluctant at first to respond to such tempting questions from Canadian journalists as 'Was there a sense that Greg was getting a bit big for his breeches?' did eventually rise to the

A confident and composed Pete Sampras (left) brought Greg Rusedski's fine run to an end while the previous page shows Andre Agassi greeting a group of terminally ill fans from Great Ormond Street Hospital, and David Luddy keeping listeners to Radio Wimbledon up to date with all the news.

A good workman, it is said, always takes particularly good care of his tools, so it will not come as a surprise to learn that Pete Sampras is meticulous when it comes to the stringing of his rackets.

And unlike anyone else in the field, the defending champion had departed from the usual instructions given to Babolat's head stringer, Jean-Claude Boldini and gone for a slightly higher tension, 32 kilos instead of 30, in response to the slightly softer balls.

The higher tension, coupled with the fact that Sampras prefers a thinner gut to most, make the Sampras rackets among the most difficult to string.

bait by admitting he 'was trying to wipe the smile off his face. It was business as usual out there. I went out and just tried to kick his ass.'

For his part, Agassi felt that he was fast reaching his peak. He overcame the unseeded Alexander Mronz from Germany 6–3, 6–3, 6–3, and gave himself ten out of ten for mental control but only nine out of ten for the way he was

hitting the ball.

Mronz surely did not notice this min imal shortcoming. 'When he has a return of serve like he did today he can do ex actly as he wants. He just hits the ball s well from the baseline and never misse There really wasn't much I could do.' Hi view was understandable. The Germa did not play badly, but once he ha recovered from 0–40 in the openin

game, Agassi was always the master.

'I felt I controlled the back of the court well and was able to wait for chances to open up the court when I wanted to without having to take a big risk,' said the number one seed, whose only seriously tricky moment of the afternoon came in the post-match interview when a woman journalist from one of the London tabloids asked him: 'Are you aware that your shorts are transparent?' 'No,' he replied, after a quizzical pause. 'But apparently you are.'

Agassi would next meet a much more menacing non-seeded opponent, Jacco Eltingh from Holland. He had already accounted for Michael Stich and Mats Wilander, and in this round was too solid and secure for seventh-seeded Wayne Ferreira, beating him 6–4, 4–6, 7–6, 6–3 in two hours 25 minutes. Eltingh, ranked 27th in the world but worthy of at least top 16 status on grass, imposed his reliable serve-and-volley

Few problems for either Boris Becker or Andre Agassi as they reached the quarter-finals.

Shuzo Matsuoka (right) produces a classic, perfectly balanced and poised backhand on his way to beating the equally unseeded Michael Joyce and becomes the first Japanese player in the quarter-finals of the men's singles for 62 years. Goran Ivanisevic (below) remained wonderfully focused as he battered Todd Martin (right) with 33 aces.

Todd Martin but still hit 33 aces [...]
Shuzo Matsuoka, next opponen[t ...]
Sampras, who easily beat fellow non[...]
Michael Joyce 6–3, 6–2, 6–4 to be[come]
the first Japanese player in the last [...]
since Kiro Sato in 1933.

Although there had been six uns[eeded]
players in the ladies' singles at the st[art of]
the day none remained by the co[...]
hour, and only three of the seeds [who]
beat them dropped a set. Two of [...]
however – Gabriela Sabatini agains[t Lisa]
Raymond and Jana Novotna ag[ainst]
Nicole Bradtke – underlined their i[ncon-]
sistency by doing so after winning [a first]
set 6–0.

Equally, Arantxa Sanchez Vi[cario]
dropped the first four games b[efore]
she pulled things round to beat [Anke]
Huber 7–5, 6–4, in what most reg[arded]
as the only really entertaining l[adies']
match of the day. Huber looked [dis-]
traught after missing an outstandin[g op-]
portunity for, in addition to taking [the]
first four games, she also held [two]
points for 5–1.

Sabatini, determined not to be c[rowded]
out as had nearly been the case i[n the]
previous round, when she trailed 0[–4 in]
the first set, swept through the op[ening]
set but Raymond took the second [and]
went on to lead 3–0 in the third [but]
missed an easy smash to make it [4–0]
when the ball landed in the tram[lines]
and the Argentinian then manag[ed to]
construct another transformation.

Meanwhile Graf dropped only [one]
game against Ines Gorrochateg[ui to]
maintain her unbeaten record in [...]
reaching the quarter-finals for the l[...]
only 14 games in eight sets. It was [look-]
ing more and more like a Graf [final]
against Sanchez or defending cham[pion]
Conchita Martinez. She followe[d a]
6–2, 6–3 defeat of Holland's Petra [Kam-]
stra (the first qualifier since the ca[reer of]
Carina Karlsson in 1984 to reach th[e last]
16 in this event) by expressing su[rprise]
that she had so far seen so little of C[entre]
Court or Court One.

Brenda Schultz-McCarthy qu[ickly]
dismissed the physically lightw[eight]

strengths and it was only through two backhand volley errors in the second set that he lost his serve for the only time in the match.

Court Two and every vantage point around it and above it was packed to see Dick Norman, the 6ft 8in lucky loser from Belgium, taking on Boris Becker. The former champion won 7–6, 6–3, 6–4 – but only after he had escaped a point for the first set at 5–6. His first re-action when he saw Norman was: 'Wow, I don't want to get into any battle with him. I want to stay cool and play tennis.'

Once that nerve-racking first set was out of the way that is precisely what he did, and he would next play Cedric Pio-line, the Frenchman who halted Petr Korda's improved performance, 7–6, 6–3, 6–2. Also through in the men's singles were the Russian, Yevgeny Kafel-nikov, an interesting, effective player, just waking up to the realisation that he could play well on grass, who outplayed Aaron Krickstein; Goran Ivanisevic, who wobbled briefly against

Yayuk Basuki from Indonesia 6–3, 6–1, but then had a shock when she reported to Court Three for the first round of the mixed doubles against Kelly Jones and Katrina Adams, only to find her partner, Murphy Jensen, was not there. Murphy, half of the most flamboyant men's doubles partnership in the world, surprisingly beaten in the first round by Stephen Noteboom and Fernon Wibier from Holland, had last been seen sitting on a couch in the transportation lounge

Gabriela Sabatini (below top), took a roller-coaster ride to victory against Lisa Raymond.

earlier that afternoon.

When he had still not made contact several hours later his absence was reported to the police, although it later transpired that he'd overslept, heard on the radio that he had been defaulted (and later fined £660) and so went to Scotland for what proved to be an abortive fishing trip before returning to the United States.

There was seldom a dull moment at Wimbledon this year.

Anke Huber ponders what might have been after she let slip a 4–0 first-set lead against the increasingly forthright Arantxa Sanchez Vicario (left).

day **8**

TUESDAY 4 JULY

Previous page: Kimiko Date draped herself with towels to keep cool in her quarter-final against Jana Novotna – but in vain. Gabriela Sabatini (right), meanwhile, let slip too many chances against Conchita Martinez.

Right: Steffi Graf was understandably overjoyed by her superb form against Mary Joe Fernandez.

Steffi Graf produced such stirring form, once into her stride, to outplay and out-class Mary Joe Fernandez in their quarter-final, but the principal concern later was whether she might have reached the peak of her form two matches too soon.

Not that Graf herself would countenance anything like that. 'No, I think that whenever I play tennis like that it doesn't matter,' she said, 'first round, last round. It's really special to be out there. It's such a joy. It's the sort of tennis you play just once in a while. Not often enough.'

It had indeed been an awesome, near-perfect second set from Graf on a day of contrasting reactions and emotions for the world of tennis – sadness at the news that Pancho Gonzales had died at his home in Las Vegas after losing his fight against cancer, but pleasure from the knowledge that Monica Seles had at last named the day when she would be announcing a firm intention to return to the circuit.

Apart from a lengthy fourth game, Graf dropped only two points in the second set of her 6–3, 6–0 defeat of the American, who in earlier rounds had started to play with growing confidence. Steffi is not easily pleased by her own performances so the obvious joy she demonstrated after this one meant it should be taken seriously. Not only did she eagerly agree with one questioner who asked her if she thought she would be unbeatable if she continued to produce such tennis, but in a quieter moment, with German writers, she actually advised them, for the first time that any of them could remember, 'to have a little bet on me'.

Yet brilliantly though Graf played in the second set, no doubt helped by the way Fernandez began with three back-hand errors and a double fault, she had made surprisingly heavy weather of the 42 minutes of the opening set. During that stage of the match the American hit many fine attacking approach shots and was willing to take the initiative at al-most every opportunity against an oppo-

nent who had beaten her in all their previous 11 matches.

This was especially so in an exhilarating final game of the first set when the Floridian bravely saved three set points before ending her challenge disappointingly with an over-hit backhand. From then on the Graf forehand was invincible to a degree that not even she often attains. Later she was still bubbling over with happiness as she mingled with the crowds and willingly signed autographs while watching her coach, Heinz Guenthardt, and Guillermo Vilas playing in the 35 and over invitation doubles. (Less happily for her, they lost to Brian Gottfried and Raul Ramirez.)

Earlier, on Centre Court, Conchita Martinez had hauled herself up from a desperately poor start – 11 forehand

'A penny for them?' Gigi Fernandez in tranquil mood as she surveys the Wimbledon scene from the dressing room window.

Conchita Martinez (near right) and Gabriela Sabatini in combat before a packed Centre Court.

errors in the first five games – to beat Gabriela Sabatini 7–5, 7–6 in a match which, from a tame beginning, became an enthralling contest, though not always for the best reasons. Martinez trailed 1–4 in the first set but then lost a 5–1 lead in the second when Sabatini suddenly began volleying with an authority and relish which she had seldom demonstrated before. Indeed, had she done so much earlier, such as when the first set was well within her grasp, there might have been a different outcome.

The crowd responded excitedly to the Argentinian's comeback, especially when she saved two match points at 2–5 and then broke back to 4–5 with a gloriously delivered backhand pass. Yet just as both players were beginning to look weary after a succession of wonderfully competitive games, which included several exhausting rallies, Sabatini began staying back again and Martinez, who produced an increasing supply of outstanding cross-court backhands, stepped up the pressure once more.

Overall, though, it was another of those frustratingly inconsistent days for Sabatini. Her serve in particular was a liability as she lost her lead in the first set which Martinez effectively won twice. On her first set point, in the 12th game, a sliced backhand from Sabatini clearly fell beyond the baseline but there was no call; umpire Jane Tabor decided it was too close a call for her to intervene.

*Safe in Daddy's arms, one of
Wimbledon's youngest visitors
in 1995 seems fascinated
by the tennis as Brenda
Schultz-McCarthy whacks a
forehand while partnering
Gabriela Sabatini.*

*No matter how hard she fought, Kimiko Date (left) could
never quite put enough pressure on Jana Novotna to create a
quarter-finals upset.*

Julie Halard and Nathalie Tauziat, seen here waiting to deal with a lob, could not cope with the Dutch and Argentine combination of power and skill, in this struggle on Court Two.

Despite her earlier moan about not having played on Centre Court since the first round, Martinez insisted that all was now well. 'I'm sure some things are up-setting me but the worst thing is for me to let them upset me. The only thing I can tell you right now is that I'm in-credibly happy to be in the semi-finals,' she said.

Just as Sabatini could have beaten Martinez, so second-seeded Arantxa Sanchez Vicario went closer to losing to Holland's Brenda Schultz-McCarthy than even the narrow enough 6–4, 7–6 scoreline indicates. At 3–3 in the first set Schultz, serving powerfully and prepared

to take risks, broke the Spaniard in the seventh game and then gave an ecstatic clenched-fist salute to her coach as if she was convinced she was well on the way to what would have been a memorable victory. The celebratory thoughts were premature. Sanchez, suddenly showing a vitality going forward, as well as from the baseline where she traditionally im-presses, took 12 of the next 13 points to win the set.

The 15th seed put the setback behind her again by breaking at the sixth time of asking in the third game of the second set, but it was still not enough to prevent the expected all-Spanish semi-final be-tween Sanchez and Martinez. 'I broke her twice and that should have been enough to win,' she said.

Sanchez was just delighted to have ad-vanced beyond her previous best effort at The Championships, while the semi-final line-up was completed when Jana Novotna beat Kimiko Date 6–2, 6–3 in a match which, perhaps not surprisingly, created far more interest back in her home country, Japan, than it did domestically.

In recent years, as the number of Japanese players making headway in world tennis has increased, so the Japan-ese media contingent has snowballed at Wimbledon and this year, when they had eleven women and two men in the draws, with both Date and Shuzo Mat-suoka reaching the quarter-finals, the ex-citement was intense.

According to Robert Guest, *The Daily Telegraph* correspondent in Tokyo, Wim-bledon was receiving 'wall-to-wall cover-age', even driving the national sumo tournament off the front pages, while on the night of Matsuoka's victory over the unseeded Michael Joyce, his exuberant lap of honour before collapsing flat on his back on the court, and the preview of Date's quarter-final, occupied the first six items on television news bulletins.

Japanese television ran late to show her match with Novotna and her compa-triot journalists cheering almost every point from the courtside. But it was not enough and, in all honesty, the slightly

built Date, who plays tennis like the most impressive lady players used to do 30–40 years earlier, was not on form. Perhaps the pressure had been too much. As one of the television men said, 'She's always in the paper and magazines now so this was more than just a tennis match for her. She had to maintain the progress of the Rising Sun.'

By now the doubles and junior events were well into their stride and in the men's doubles the holders, Todd Woodbridge and Mark Woodforde, became involved in a domestic set-to in more ways than one before winning their quarter-final against fellow Australians, Mark Philippoussis and Patrick Rafter. The Woodies' won 6–2, 1–6, 6–2, 7–6. At the end there were angry exchanges as Woodbridge was severely rebuked by Rafter for something he had apparently said which led to his girl friend leaving the court in tears. And in a major upset Americans Rick Leach and Scott Melville beat Holland's top-seeded Jacco Eltingh and Paul Haarhuis.

With their singles duty done for the day, it was not only winners Sanchez and Novotna who went back on court to beat Katrina Adams and Zina Garrison-Jackson but also two of the vanquished singles quarter-finalists, Sabatini and Schultz, joined forces to continue their doubles progress against Julie Halard and Nathalie Tauziat.

In the mixed doubles, where every appearance by Martina Navratilova and Jonathan Stark was becoming a star attraction – on this occasion they had an impressively clear-cut 6–3, 6–3 win over Rick Leach and Natasha Zvereva – Court One also rang to the sound of much excitement and eventually a standing ovation as the British pair, Mark Petchey and Clare Wood, reached the last eight with a 6–4, 7–5 defeat of the Americans, T.J. Middleton and Lori McNeil. It offered some compensation to the home crowd for the 6–4, 6–2 defeat of Jamie Delgado, 18, by the Croatian Zeljko Krajan.

Delgado, a leading British junior since winning the national 12 and under

grass-court title in 1989, struggled with his first serve and too many volleying errors against a harder-serving opponent who was encouraged by Goran Ivanisevic's supportive presence beside Court Nine. It meant that of the eleven Britons who had started out in the junior singles, Martin Lee stood alone in the third round. He continued his excellent summer with 52 minutes of studiously concentrated and efficient left-hander serve-and-volleying to beat the dangerous Jean-Baptiste Perlant of France. Alex Osterrieth from Biggin Hill should have joined him but missed a volley on match point against Israel's Amir Hadad.

Britain's Martin Lee continued his surge into the top ten of the world junior rankings with a splendidly efficient win to reach the last 16 of the boys' singles.

WIMBLEDON

day **9**

WEDNESDAY 5 JULY

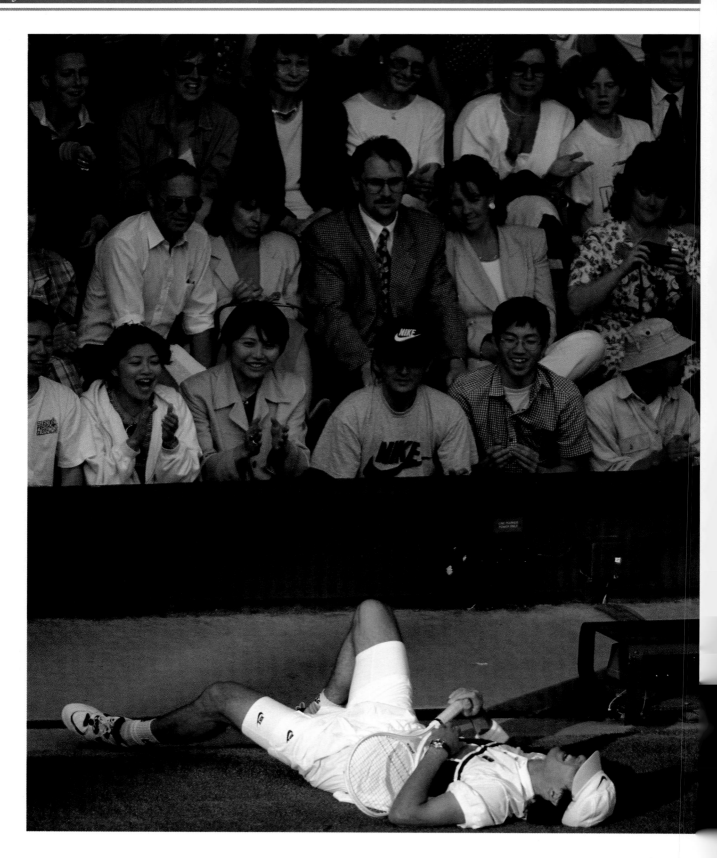

On the eve of the men's singles quarter-finals, there had been reports that book-makers all over Europe and in Asia were being inundated by customers eager to bet that unseeded Frenchman, Cedric Pioline, would beat Boris Becker. Some-one, it seemed, had been spreading alarming rumours that Becker's calf muscle injury was more of a problem than anyone was prepared to admit. Pioline very nearly did win, but in a magnificent match, with both players totally oblivious to extraneous events which had started to veer out of control and not really understanding what it all meant when told about such financial shenanigans later. Becker devised a brilliant escape which not only saved the bookmakers around £400,000 in Britain alone but must have gone down pretty well with the Wimbledon seeding committee as well.

For the semi-final line-up which Becker's late-night victory then completed, read Andre Agassi v. Becker; Pete Sampras v. Goran Ivanisevic, just as they had predicted. Not only that, but their calculations for the women's singles had

been just as exemplary. They had been right on one or other of the events, through to the semi-final stages, a few times before but this was the first time since seeding began in 1927 that they could boast such a record for both.

The drama of Becker's 6–3, 6–1, 6–7, 6–7, 9–7 victory was quite remarkable, for although he had only once before lost a match in which he had taken the first two sets, it certainly looked, when he was break down in the fifth, that the even bigger-hitting Frenchman would win. As he began to calm down, after walking off Court One with a standing ovation ringing in his ears, Becker said, 'It was a wonderful Wimbledon moment for me to win a match in which the emotions had been running so high.'

When he had romped through the first two sets, there was no hint of what was to follow. 'Pioline raised his game to a very high level,' said Becker, 'but even when I was a set down in the fifth, I still had that desire to win – and that was the bottom line.' It certainly made for the most exhilarating match so far in The Championships.

'One of the articles in the paper this time said I was short, fat, bald and ugly. I didn't get that criticism a few years ago.'
Andre Agassi on the changing tone of newspaper coverage since he won Wimbledon in 1992

A match and many moments to savour as Boris Becker dives for a spectacular forehand volley cross-court winner which floored Cedric Pioline (left). Those who had wined and dined out by candlelight and round bonfires overnight before joining the massive queues for the men's quarter-final matches (as shown on the previous pages) were handsomely rewarded.

Shuzo Matsuoka (below) did not yield easily to Pete Sampras, but Yevgeny Kafelnikov (right) too often lacked experience at this level in key moments against Goran Ivanisevic.

Pioline, who had achieved little since finishing runner-up at the US Open in 1993, apart from changing his coach twice and redesigning his forehand, was getting nowhere until a sudden and considerable tactical switch, when he was two sets down in less than an hour, produced one of the epics of the year, as well as the 1995 championships. At one stage in the second set the Frenchman needed assistance from the trainer for an abdominal injury, and he later revealed that at the start of the third set he'd thought about retiring. 'I felt pain. I couldn't serve, I was just pushing the ball. But then I hit some good shots from the baseline and told myself, "OK, let's go. This is a Wimbledon quarter-final. Let's see if I can take it to a tie-break and then see what happens." I had a bit of luck on a few points and the match turned.'

Clawing his way back from the brink of defeat he won the next two sets in tie-breaks, but without breaking the serve of Becker, who had recovered from 1–6 to 6–6 in the first of them before wasting the recovery and holding his first match point at 10–9 in the second tie-break which settled the fourth set. Pioline, supporting fine serves with occasional sharp volleys but mostly blistering returns on both flanks, saved it with a service winner and moved into a fifth set where he broke for 2–1 but then played a rare mishit backhand to lose his advantage in the eighth game.

As the final set score mounted and both men in turn created and missed great opportunities, the atmosphere was intense. Becker netted a backhand under pressure on his second match point at 5–4, while Pioline escaped the third with another of those stunning passes and the fourth when Becker chased in behind a second serve return only for the next Pioline shot to clip the net and bounce over the former champion's racket.

Becker finally won after four hours 11 minutes when Pioline missed two backhand volleys, and so kept alive his hopes of marking the tenth anniversary of his first Wimbledon title with his fourth – although the next battle against Andre Agassi he could expect to be tougher still.

The pigeon-toed guy in the baggy white shorts described his form as he dismissed Jacco Eltingh 6–2, 6–3, 6–4 as 'his best so far'. Although he trailed 1–3 in the third set, it was generally a virtuoso performance of astonishingly consistent power, control and hand–eye co-ordination.

'Everything is coming together for me at the right time,' said Agassi, with the confidence of Mystic Meg recommending what numbers to choose in the National Lottery. 'This is the biggest tournament in the world. If you can win only one, you pick this one. The Centre Court has the greatest environment in the world.'

The other semi-final would be a repeat of the previous year's final, Pete Sampras (who went a set down and was 0–40 at 3–3 in the second before turning things round against Shuzo Matsuoka), against Goran Ivanisevic. The Croatian hit another 33 aces in three sets, taking his total in five matches to 137 as he beat the sixth-seeded Russian, Yevgeny Kafelnikov, who many experts tout as a future world number one. The contest, which Ivanisevic won 7–5, 7–6, 6–3, turned on a thrilling 24-point tie-break in which Kafelnikov four times held set point before yielding at 13–11 on his opponent's third.

'I didn't like the way things were going,' observed Sampras, in that wonderful manner he has of understating things, as he reflected on those three break points which could have left Matsuoka serving for 5–3 in the second set of their attractive match on Court One. It was hardly surprising. Sampras had found himself playing and completely missing when trying to make contact with a swirling Japanese serve on the fourth point of the match – and the crowd could hardly contain its surprise or excitement as, for the best part of two sets, the 107th-ranked underdog virtually matched the champion shot for shot.

FRED
1934

JOHN
1935

PERRY
1936

Chris Evert and her husband, former Olympic skier Andy Mill, introduce four-year-old son Alex to the action, as Boris Becker's wife Barbara and his coach, Nick Bollettieri, anxiously follow his fluctuating and dramatic contest with Cedric Pioline. Fans pay a touching tribute to the late Fred Perry, whose wit, wisdom and charismatic presence were so clearly missed.

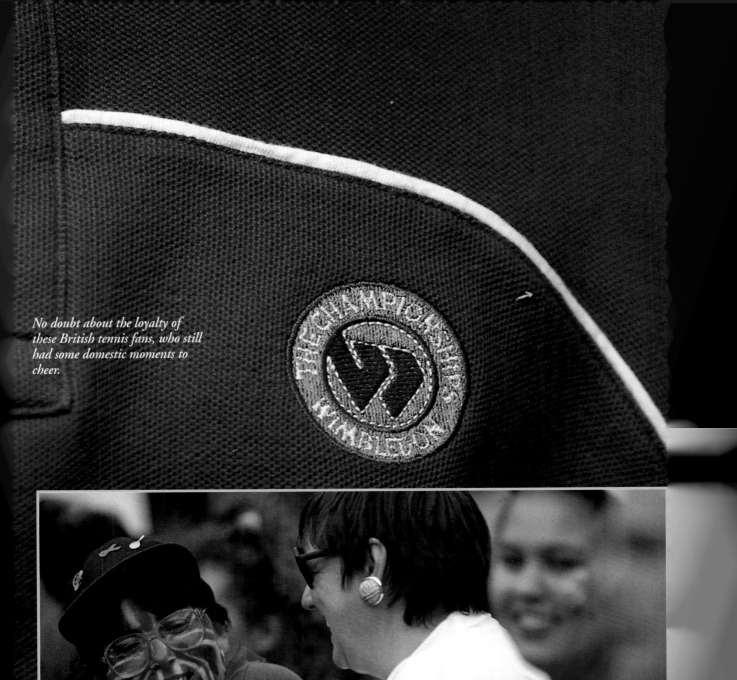

No doubt about the loyalty of these British tennis fans, who still had some domestic moments to cheer.

Even in defeat, Mark Petchey and Clare Wood provided late night British interest and excitement on Centre Court.

Sampras, though, had another gear in reserve and from 0–40 in that forever crucial seventh game took 12 consecutive points to lead 5–3, 40–0. 'Even if I'd broken in that most important game I don't think I would have won,' said Matsuoka, who had taken an injury delay while the trainer removed an insect from his eye. 'But maybe it would have been a closer match.' Sampras knew that was true. 'I need to improve by more than 15 per cent if I'm to stay in the tournament,' he said, still not content with the level of his serve.

While Steffi Graf was able to rest, at least in terms of match play in preparation for her singles semi-final the fol-

lowing day, her three remaining rivals for the crown were being kept busy in doubles. Arantxa Sanchez Vicario and Jana Novotna, playing together, beat Pam Shriver and Nicole Arendt 7–6, 7–5. Conchita Martinez and Patricia Tarabini went out to the holders, Gigi Fernandez and Natasha Zvereva 6–2, 6–1.

British interest in the mixed doubles ended when, despite a magnificent fight, Mark Petchey and Clare Wood were beaten 6–2, 7–6 by two of the biggest hitters in the game, Grant Connell and Lindsay Davenport. But domestic hopes remained in the boys' singles where Martin Lee, showing tenacity and coolness in

fighting back from being a break down in the second set and then 0–4 in the tie-break, beat Holland's Peter Wessels 6–3, 7–6.

Supported by a large Court 13 crowd, among them Buster Mottram, Britain's last boys' singles finalist when beaten by Bjorn Borg in 1972, Lee delighted with his touch, as well as his aggression round the net.

Lindsay Davenport's spirits and her tennis soon lifted up again with help from her mixed doubles partner, Grant Connell.

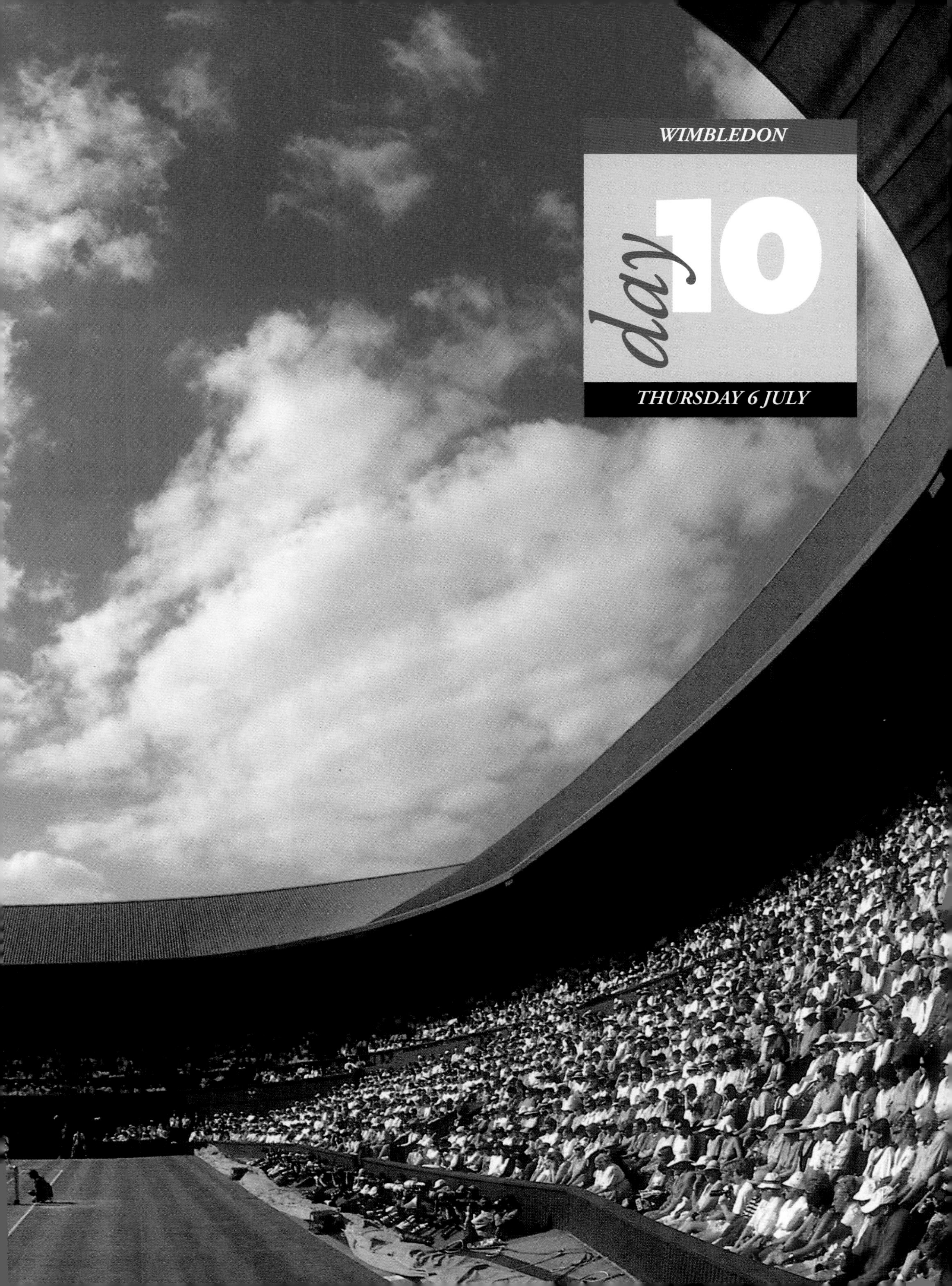

WIMBLEDON

day 10

THURSDAY 6 JULY

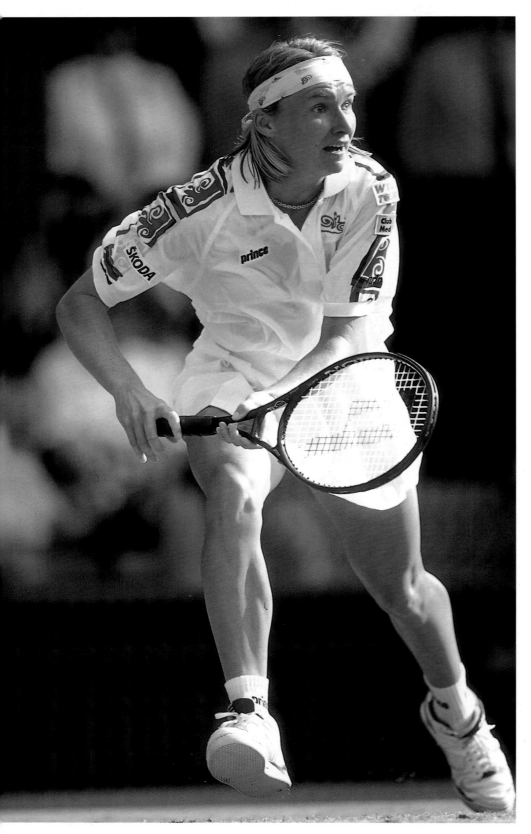

No tears this time from Jana Novotna as once again her dream of winning Wimbledon was thwarted by Steffi Graf – just understandable disappointment that not even one of her best performances against the world number one had been enough to bring her victory in the semifinals. This time there was no need for recriminations either.

One could hardly fault Novotna's tactics. As often as possible she denied Graf the pace for the counter-hitting which is her forte, and she frequently opened up the court to finish off points. 'I really believe that if I'd played this way against anyone else I'd have been the winner, but Steffi is always able to raise her game. She never gives up and is very tough to finish off,' Novotna said when finally forced to a 5–7, 6–4, 6–2 defeat after two hours two minutes.

Novotna insisted that the memory of that heart-breaking 1993 final, when she let slip a 4–1, 40–30 lead in the final set against Graf and then broke down and wept on the compassionate shoulder of HRH the Duchess of Kent at the presentation ceremony, never crossed her mind. 'Today I felt was going to be my day,' she said firmly.

Yet all credit to Graf who, for the first time in the fortnight, needed to tap into her vast reservoir of mental resilience and was repeatedly able to play herself out of critical situations on a day when she had begun so nervously and erratically. She missed so many groundstrokes on both flanks and demonstrated so little authority on her serve that one could hardly believe that this was the same player who had dropped only five games in her three previous matches.

Two break points were crucially saved at 2–2 in the second set, which had begun with Graf actually believing briefly that she was going to be beaten. Two more break points, the first of them with the help of a bad bounce, were saved at 3–3. Steffi, who had to be given painkillers for a headache one game after that, said: 'Things didn't look very good for quite some time, so obviously I'm happy to have turned it round.'

For long periods it was almost as if the crowd, though gripped by the way the contest unfolded, was reluctant to express its feelings because there was so much uncertainty over which way a match of such variety would go. This was underlined in the climax to the second set: Novotna went down on her knees as she broke back from love to 4–5 with a brilliant low backhand volley, but then lost her own serve to love and the next seven points on the way to trailing 0–2 in the third set.

Even when leading 4–2 in the final set, Graf still had to work for her points against an opponent who cleverly gave her no rhythm and still had two chances to break back in the seventh game.

In the end, however, Graf rounded things off in fine style with a classic forehand winner which made it match point and then a backhand down the line timed to perfection. The victory increased her career record against Novotna, probably the most gifted player in the women's game not to have won a Grand Slam title, to 24–3.

Against Arantxa Sanchez Vicario, whom she already knew would be her opponent in her seventh Wimbledon final, the record was 25–8. Yet as Graf said, as she reflected on the second seed's 6–3, 6–7, 6–1 defeat of fellow Spaniard, Conchita Martinez, 'I won't be underestimating Sanchez at all because she played well and could have won more easily.'

That was true. And certainly Sanchez played with greater zest, willingness and conviction than many thought possible on a surface where hitherto she had not looked over-ambitious. Against that, however, rarely can any champion have defended her title with so little conviction as Martinez. Her later admission that, after drawing level in the second set, 'I felt I could probably win but I didn't believe enough' said it all.

Martinez certainly had her problems, first with her game and then with blisters on both feet, which somehow enabled her to take not just one injury time-out but two. Although she looked strong and positive enough when rescuing the second set – after Sanchez had let her back in by becoming tentative when leading 5–2 and then 4–1 in the tie-break – that rasping backhand which had contributed so much to Martinez's triumph a year earlier was the shot which, this time, so often let her down.

Once more Steffi Graf is all smiles after fending off one of the strongest, most consistent and sustained challenges she had faced from Jana Novotna (left) who, though beaten, had much to cherish from the way she had played.

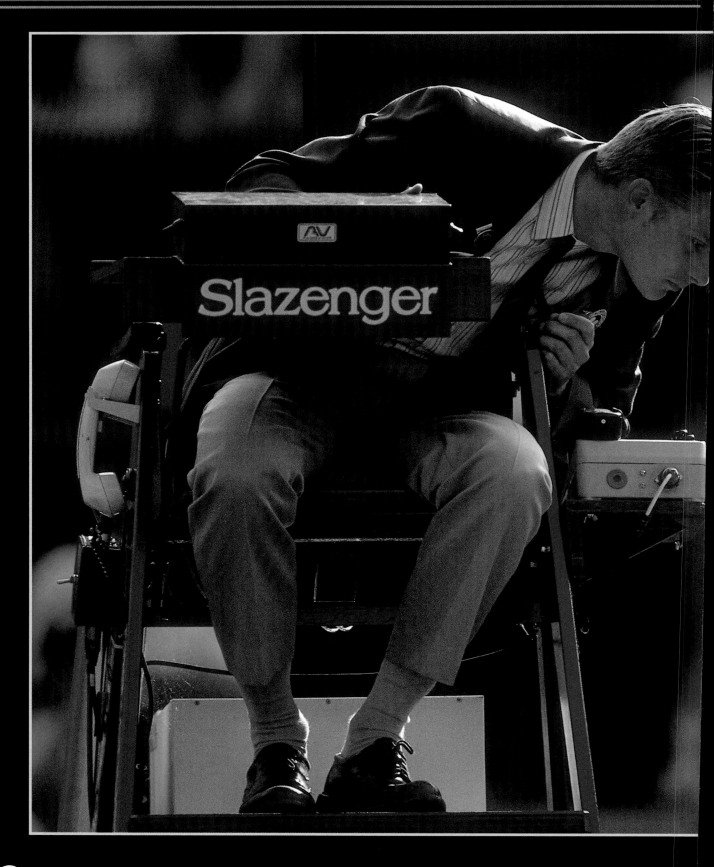

This is not a sight one often sees – Steffi Graf offering more than a quizzical look when she disagrees with a line-call. Here, umpire Andreas Egli from Switzerland listens as she states her case.

The anxiety in her face was reflected in her tennis as defending champion Conchita Martinez (below) was knocked out in the semi-finals by an ecstatic fellow Spaniard, Arantxa Sanchez Vicario.

In the final set it was, as the score suggests, all Sanchez, gloriously mixing lobs, drop shots and even an occasional drive volley into a game which suddenly looked as if, perhaps, Graf might have more on her plate in the final than almost anyone had supposed. Sanchez, scurrying and harassing in a way which had been missing at both the Australian Open and the French Open, called her presence in the final 'a dream come true' and added: 'It's a great feeling, I have nothing to lose.'

Checking the men's doubles honours board, it had clearly not escaped the notice of Todd Woodbridge and Mark Woodforde that the only partnership which had won the title three years in succession in the Open era was that of Tony Roche and John Newcombe, still together as joint captains of the Australian Davis Cup team. The 'Woodies', winners in 1993 and 1994, moved closer to equalling their achievement when they smartly dismissed Mark Knowles of the Bahamas and Daniel Nestor of Canada 6–3, 6–3, 6–3 in one hour 29 minutes.

who used his greater speed and agility to break service twice in each set and then finished the contest with a typically extravagant backhand cross-court return after two match points had been saved.

'He's got a wonderful schooling in the school of hard knocks,' said Ian Barclay, Lee's coach at the Rover LTA School at Bisham Abbey. 'You can't buy experience. You have to learn the hard way.' Yet, as everyone was soon to be reminded, Wimbledon '95 was not over for Lee. He and James Trotman were still alive in the boys' doubles.

Anna Kournikova (left) provided renewed evidence of her outstanding youthful talent and power as she reached the semi-finals of the junior girls' singles at the expense of Mi-Ra Jeon of South Korea.

The second semi-final was suspended due to failing light, with Yevgeny Kafelnikov and Marc Goellner leading Rick Leach and Scott Melville 6–3, 6–7, 7–6 after two hours. Leach, who won Wimbledon with Jim Pugh in 1990, and Melville, making his Wimbledon doubles debut, took the second-set tie-break 14–12 on their fourth set point after saving four against them.

Woodforde later teamed up with Larisa Neiland to sweep into the semi-finals of the mixed doubles with a 6–2, 6–1 defeat of the Australian duo, Andrew Florent and Catherine Barclay. Martina Navratilova and Jonathan Stark also ran out of daylight and had their quarter-final against Sandon Stolle and Mary Joe Fernandez halted at one set all.

In the juniors, Japan's Haruka Inoue, who had upset top-seeded Yvette Basting from Holland in the second round, continued her progress into the semi-finals, as did the foot-stampingly defiant 14-year-old Anna Kournikova, after being a break down in the final set against 1994 runner-up, Mi-Ra Jeon from Korea.

Martin Lee's encouraging run ended when the 17-year-old, who had already gone one round further than his ninth seeding demanded, lost disappointingly 6–2, 6–3 to Mexico's Alejandro Hernandez. Lee, though trying hard, was kept under constant pressure by the third seed,

Andre Agassi's actress girlfriend, Brooke Shields, is all too aware that things have turned against him in his semi-final against Boris Becker.

By the time those who had popped out for tea between the men's singles semi-finals returned to their places, everything most of them had been expecting was going to plan. Pete Sampras had lifted his form in the right way, in the right place and certainly at the right time, to stave off a tremendous challenge from Goran Ivanisevic, who must have felt that this was probably his best chance to date of upsetting the American on grass. Then, hitting returns with such consistent ferocity that his opponent must have felt that he was trying to counter some supreme power from Outer Space, Andre Agassi, who had romped away with the first set in 33 minutes, went into a 4–1 lead in the second with four more astonishing groundstroke winners which also gave him a second service break.

In the minds of most people at that moment, the dream final – Agassi v. Sampras, number one v. number two in the world, the 1992 champion against the player who'd succeeded to the title in 1993 and held it in 1994 – was beginning to look like reality. Not, though, to Boris Becker, the man who had been on the receiving end of Agassi's assault.

One game later, he moved to break point against Agassi for the first time in a rally of 19 strokes, the longest in an exhilarating afternoon, and he followed that up with a forehand cross-court winner to make it 2–4. Becker then held up his arms to the crowd, as if to tell them what he told everyone else later: 'Never underestimate me at Wimbledon.'

Agassi, despite spells in the fourth set when he looked close to regaining his commanding influence in the first, was never quite the same again, while Becker, bounding ever more eagerly from point to point and producing more than enough aces (22) to counteract the flurry of double faults which appeared alarmingly, also in the gripping fourth set, suddenly had the look of a winner about him.

No doubt the date had proved an added inspiration to him. It was ten years to the day since, aged 17 and unseeded, he had won Wimbledon for the first time and become the youngest men's singles champion. The prize for winning this match, over and above pride and an enormous boost to the confidence of a player many regarded as past his prime, would be his first Grand Slam tournament final since 1991 and the chance to become Wimbledon champion for a fourth time.

From looking as businesslike and efficient as possible for someone who shuffles about the court like he does, in garb which almost defies description, Agassi became lethargic – almost numbed, in terms of mobility and strategy – while Becker leapt, literally sometimes, at the opportunity to take charge. The second set was still the pivotal part of the match, though no longer for the same reason. Instead of securing Agassi's authority, it provided Becker with his launchpad. From 1–4 he moved ahead to 5–4, and although Agassi managed to take it to a tie-break, his lame backhand on the second point followed by a stupendous reflex forehand volley from Becker on the sixth sped the German to a rousing 7–1 margin.

A double fault followed by Agassi making a dreadful hash of a smash to lose his serve in the seventh game was the turning point in the third set, while the fourth, with both men producing moments of their best and worst points, became a thrilling cat-and-mouse affair as first one and then the other had break points. Agassi, for instance, survived four in the first game and three in the third, Becker at least one in each of his first four service games on the way to another tie-break – although it was the glaring opportunity which Agassi missed for a winning pass that would have put him 5–3 ahead which was the most significant.

Once into the fourth-set tie-break Becker surely sensed that the match would be his. 'I've had plenty of recent practice on tie-breaks,' he said, in a

Boris Becker's game, which suddenly took off in explosive fashion from a set and 1–4 down, enabled him to push Andre Agassi into the background in the semi-finals.

grinning reference to his marathon survival against Cedric Pioline on Court One two evenings earlier. The look of despair on the face of Agassi's coach, Brad Gilbert, when the American over-hit a forehand on the first point only increased as Becker, with aces on the third and sixth points, plus another piece of

wonderful net covering to punch away a volley on the seventh, was unstoppable. In normal circumstances Agassi would never have over-hit the forehand which ended the match and gave Becker another 7–1 tie-break – but neither mentally nor physically did he have anything left to give. It had been Wimbledon's best match of the year and Becker's best match anywhere for far longer than that.

Sampras had been so impressed by the way Shuzo Matsuoka had bowed to the crowd in traditional Japanese fashion at the end of their quarter-final that he decided to celebrate his 7–6, 4–6, 6–3, 4–6, 6–3 victory over Ivanisevic in similar, if somewhat self-conscious fashion. Yet the fact that he did so underlined the American's satisfaction with the way he had played in a match which, for most of its two hours 34 minutes, provided grass-court tennis at its best – and a bending of Pete Sampras's natural reserve.

True, Ivanisevic struck 38 aces, taking his total for the tournament to 142 in six matches. But unlike their final a year earlier, this was not boring and the Croatian certainly didn't fold the way he had done after losing the first set on that occasion.

The pattern was set in the thrilling first game, in which Sampras served three aces but was also beaten three times by stunning Ivanisevic passing shots, only for Goran to miss what looked poised to be another, on the first critical break point he had engineered. Although there were some blunders worthy of blushes, most of the 'errors' were forced by the brilliance of the other man, so it was appropriate that the first set went to a tie-break where Sampras, despite leading 6–4, still needed four set points to finish it off.

Basically Ivanisevic was beaten this time not because he lost heart but through loss of concentration. That was underlined when, having levelled in the second set without dropping a single point on his serve, and starting the third set with an ace, he then double-faulted twice and was broken to 15 while still

'When you're playing Goran, it's like riding a roller-coaster . . . It's up to you to stay as solid as possible.'

Pete Sampras, after his match against the giant Croatian

fretting about those mistakes. Perhaps, too, the adrenalin was still pumping too fast after the memorable final point of that second set. Sampras had failed to put the ball away at the first attempt, but valiantly resisted the first two Ivanisevic attempts to blast first a forehand and then a backhand drive through him at the net before yielding on the third, when the power of the shot almost jolted him off his feet.

Similarly, though, at the start of the fifth set Ivanisevic again faltered when he was consistently holding serve with far greater ease than his opponent, and the initiative might have stayed with him. On the other hand, the way Sampras pounced at 30–30 in the second game with a wonderful lunging forehand volley, and intimidated Ivanisevic sufficiently with his next return for the first volley to be put wide, confirmed his extra experience and class.

'When you're playing Goran, it's like riding a roller-coaster,' said Sampras. 'He has by far the biggest serve in the game, possibly in the history of the game, so you just have to make sure you don't get discouraged by all those aces whizzing past you because you also know that between his good shots he can hit some bad shots. It is up to you to stay as solid as possible.'

Once again the focus of mixed doubles attention was on Martina Navratilova, as she and Jonathan Stark won twice during the day to give her the chance for a 19th Wimbledon title. Having completed their quarter-final, interrupted overnight because of bad light, by recovering from a break down to beat Sandon Stolle and Mary Joe Fernandez 7–6, 3–6, 6–3, they then staged another revival in the semi-finals to beat two more of the world's best doubles players, Mark Woodforde and Larisa Neiland.

Also through to the final were Cyril Suk and Gigi Fernandez, who defeated Grant Connell and Lindsay Davenport after Fernandez had earlier made her regular date for a place with Natasha

Zvereva in the final of the women's doubles, in a 7–6, 6–7, 6–2 win over Neiland and the American, Meredith McGrath. Once again the champions in the three previous years were to find Jana Novotna and Arantxa Sanchez Vicario waiting for them – but only just. The Czech Republic–Spanish combination were pushed to the limit before they overcame a wilting Gabriela Sabatini and Brenda Schultz-McCarthy, 7–6, 6–7, 6–4.

Meanwhile upsets continued in the juniors, with second-seeded Anna Kournikova, the 14-year-old Florida-based Russian, who already knows how to congratulate herself on winners in English but expresses annoyance or frustration in her native tongue, losing to the much bigger and stronger Tamarine Tanasugarn from Thailand 7–6, 6–3. That meant the 15th and 9th seeds (Aleksandra Olsza from Poland) were through to the final. In the boys' singles, however, Germany's Nicolas Kiefer justified his top seeding and qualified to dispute the title with unseeded Olivier Mutis of France, who had three of his five matches go to three sets.

The ups and downs for Pete Sampras, who was stretched to five sets by Goran Ivanisevic.

The final of the ladies' singles at Wimbledon is always a special occasion, but few could have envisaged just how special and memorable the climax to what had hitherto been a mainly modest competition in 1995 would be.

On past performances Steffi Graf, recognised as the best player in the world on grass, should have been looking forward to a testing but not particularly exacting challenge as she sought her sixth title in eight years. Arantxa Sanchez Vicario, after all, had never before gone beyond the quarter-finals at an event which had not generally been at the top of her target list. Not only that, but she had won only eight of her 33 matches against the German, who had beaten her in the French Open four weeks earlier and went into the match unbeaten in 31 matches during the year. The bookmakers decided Graf was the 3–1 odds-on favourite.

What was to unfold, however, in the two hours two minutes which followed the cracking forehand winner which Graf unleashed on the very first point, to set the pace and pattern, was not just the best women's final but the finest women's match anyone could remember. That included the epic marathon in which Margaret Court eventually wore down Billie Jean King in 1970, which probably sustained a higher quality but not the emotional roller-coaster ride on which Graf and Sanchez took everyone.

It had everything in abundance, great competitive winners, constant fluctuations in fortunes, courage, conviction and total commitment, culminating in an incredible eleventh game of the final set which lasted 20 minutes and spanned 32 points. Sanchez held eight game points but Graf finally took it with a blistering forehand drive into the corner on her sixth game point, moments after setting up the chance with a brilliant volley which ended another fierce hitting and retrieving rally of 12 shots.

The game will surely be as memorable as the Bjorn Borg–John McEnroe tie-break in the 1980 men's singles final – and everyone, including the two players and countless millions watching on tele-

vision round the world, guessed that it would prove decisive. So it proved, for although Graf was even more tired at that point than her opponent, and cannot have been helped by being foot-faulted on her first delivery as she began serving out for the match, the adrenalin was also pumping faster than ever to carry her through.

The Sanchez exhaustion was more in her heart than in those legs which for so long had been helping her to retrieve and return almost everything the German produced. Here was a player who had increasingly won the admiration and affection of the crowd for boldly adopting tactics which were essentially foreign to her. Indeed, if only through her sheer resilience and exuberance, she contributed even more than Graf to lifting the match to such a peak of excitement and intensity.

Graf, despite that crunching first point, looked nervous early on and it showed when, from 15–0 in the seventh game and then disturbed by a call, she made four consecutive forehand errors to give Sanchez the break for 4–3 and, because of that, the set. In the past Sanchez has been rated highly for her terrier-like refusal to give way under pressure, but not so much for her initiative or ingenuity. On this occasion, though, despite twice being broken in the second set, she looked rich in both qualities, and as the third set developed it really began to look as if her extra aggression would be rewarded.

Although Graf could and should have taken command after breaking for 2–1, helped by a superb forehand winner struck on the run from close to the net cord judge, she let Sanchez back in from 30–0 in the next game with four unforced errors, the last of them a double fault – and from then on it was almost anybody's guess how it would go.

When Sanchez survived two more break points in the fifth game she punched the air with a gesture of continuing defiance and determination. And with the Graf forehand, which had earned her so such success in the past, going through a spell when it threatened

The rallies were long, the competition fierce and the atmosphere almost unbelievably intense before Steffi Graf regained the trophy to become champion for a sixth time, despite a brilliant performance by Arantxa Sanchez Vicario.

Steffi Graf's relief, as well as joy, was obvious as she accepted congratulations from a resilient opponent, acknowledged the cheers of the crowd and then shared her tearful happiness with family and friends.

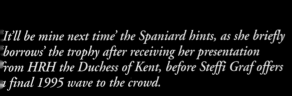

'It'll be mine next time' the Spaniard hints, as she briefly 'borrows' the trophy after receiving her presentation from HRH the Duchess of Kent, before Steffi Graf offers a final 1995 wave to the crowd.

to be her downfall, the tension was incredible. One moment you felt certain that a new champion was about to be crowned, the next that Graf's experience would continue to pull her out of every crisis. It was not only great tennis but great theatre, in every sense.

As for that eleventh game of the final set, Graf said: 'I've never been involved in anything like it and never, probably, has one game ever meant as much at such a stage of the match. I think that it definitely produced the best tennis from both of us. Nobody gave up. We both really tried. We were both going for it. Many of the points were fantastic.'

Some of the forehand cross-court winners by Sanchez in that game not only beat Graf for pace but deceived her with their guile as well. But for a couple of tentative volleys, one especially on her fifth game point, she might not have needed, jokingly, to grab the winner's trophy out of Graf's hand and given the German hers instead, for a few seconds before they took their final bows at the end of the presentation ceremony. It would probably have been hers by right.

At the end, instead of taking her customary jog straight over to beneath the players' box to stretch up and take congratulations from her family, Graf took the long way round, right up into the stand, to hug them one by one with tears streaming down her face. The reaction was understandable. Wimbledon means so much to her. Although she had done her utmost to play down the extent to which she still felt threatened by a chronic back injury, this was the moment when she could no longer hold back the emotion.

'It's been a difficult few weeks,' she said. 'Sometimes you don't think you can make it through.' She declined to elaborate or speculate on how long she can continue to overcome an injury which might, it seems, end her career at any time. This was a time to relish the present, not to worry about the future, although she left no doubt as to her attitude.

'I do hope and I do have the feeling that I'll be back next year. I really count on that,' added an outstanding champion, whose success placed her level on Wimbledon singles titles with Billie Jean King. She is now headed only by Helen Wills Moody with eight and Martina Navratilova with nine.

For Sanchez, who had every reason to be proud of her performance and confident in her ability possibly to go one step further next time, there was still some other Centre Court business to be undertaken. There was still a sizeable crowd present when she returned, with Jana Novotna, nearly three hours after the end of the singles, for the final of the women's doubles against Gigi Fernandez and Natasha Zvereva, hoping to triumph for a fourth consecutive year. The spectators were again handsomely rewarded.

Many of the short-range volley exchanges were breathtakingly lengthy as well as spectacular, with Sanchez still full of energy – but the light ran out on them at 4–4 in the final set. The original suggestion was that they would resume on Court One the next day, at the same time that the men's singles was to begin on Centre Court, for Fernandez would also be needed for the final of the mixed doubles which would follow Sampras v. Becker.

Fernandez, however, had a much better idea. She agreed to complete the women's doubles final where it had started, and certainly where it belonged, on Centre Court and then go straight on with the mixed.

In between the two Sanchez appearances, the old firm of Todd Woodbridge and Mark Woodforde managed to do what even John McEnroe and Peter Fleming never achieved, by winning the men's doubles for three years in succession. The previous partnership to do so had been fellow Australians, John Newcombe and Tony Roche, between 1968 and 1970 – and on the day that the old timers were retaining the invitation 45 and over doubles title with a 6–4, 7–5

Bob Hewitt and Frew McMillan provide happy reminders of the doubles skill which made them champions in 1967 and 1972 but it was not quite enough in their 45 and over invitation semi-final against their regular foes and fellow former champions, John Newcombe and Tony Roche.

defeat of Owen Davidson and Cliff Drysdale, there was a bottle of champagne on ice from Roche waiting for their successors to be toasted when they returned to the dressing room.

Woodbridge and Woodforde won 7–5, 7–6, 7–6 in a mainly dour, serve-dominated contest, in which there was just one break of serve in the opening set and a double fault from Melville which enabled the holders to move ahead 5–3 in the third-set tie-break.

As always the coaches – and representatives of management companies – were evident for the finals of the junior singles. Olivier Mutis, the unseeded Frenchman who had knocked out three seeds along the way, completed a memorable week for him by taking full advantage of

too many unforced errors from top-seeded German, Nicolas Kiefer, to win 6–2, 6–2, while Aleksandra Olsza, the only Polish player in any event, also became the first player from that country to win a title during the fortnight, by beating Thailand's Tamarine Tanasugarn 7–5, 7–6.

The day on which Virginia Wade and Wendy Turnbull also retained the 35 and over doubles also set up the all-too-rare opportunity for a British junior success. One year after Lizzie Jelfs enjoyed a share in the junior girls' doubles, Martin Lee, 17, and James Trotman, 17, combined magnificently to upset the far more experienced Americans, Justin Gimelstob and Ryan Wolters 6–4, 2–6, 6–3 to reach the final of the boys' doubles.

It's no wonder that the crowds still flock to watch them when champions from the past clearly enjoy themselves as much as Virginia Wade and Wendy Turnbull, seen here celebrating their successful defence of the ladies' 35 and over invitation doubles.

Overleaf: Rick Leach puts away an overhead shot, but he and Scott Melville could not prevent Mark Woodforde (foreground left) and Todd Woodbridge becoming only the second pair to win the men's doubles title three years in succession.

Barbara Becker could not bear to watch as her husband's bid for the men's singles title crumbled – although the crowd still demanded that he took a lap of honour.

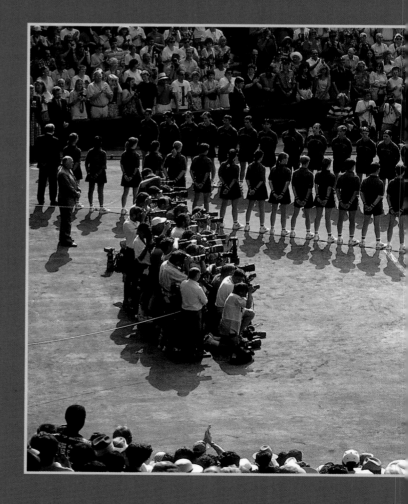

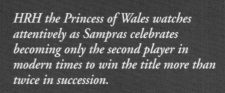

HRH the Princess of Wales watches attentively as Sampras celebrates becoming only the second player in modern times to win the title more than twice in succession.

Momentarily, when Boris Becker won the first set in a tie-break, there was the possibility of a German double again at The Championships – but not for long. The thoroughness and confidence with which Pete Sampras soon established himself firmly in control, to win the men's singles title for a third consecutive time, suggested that he was even capable of going on to threaten Bjorn Borg's unbeaten record spanning the five years from 1976 to 1980.

'I used to own the Centre Court but he owns it now,' said Becker who, though disappointed that his dream of celebrating a fourth title on the tenth anniversary of his first had evaporated, acknowledged what he called the American's 'very amazing feat. Very few players have played against me the way he did today.'

Once Sampras broke Becker for the first of five times in the third game of the second set, such was his developing supremacy that it became more a clinical demonstration of grass-court perfection than a contest to match the drama of the ladies' final the day before. It lasted just two hours 28 minutes before Sampras raised his arms aloft to mark a 6–7, 6–2, 6–4, 6–2 victory which brought as much joy to his coach, Tim Gullikson, forced to remain at home in Chicago as a television viewer while continuing his fight against cancer.

There was the usual criticism that, apart from the first set, the tennis was so predictable that it was boring. Yet even those who find such technical and powerful skill monotonous must surely have admired the masterly perfection which Sampras brings to so many facets of his game. Certainly there was not the mass exodus for tea, evident in the previous year's final.

Sampras, for the second successive year, did not drop his serve and this time there was not even a break point against him, with only two of his service games even going to deuce. His returns, especially as Becker curiously persisted in serving to his backhand, scored freely,

while his first volleys were sharper than they had been anywhere in the 12 months since the 1994 final.

The IBM match statistics told it all. In the 16 categories they study, Sampras came out top in all but two of them.

Once the first set was over, Boris Becker simply could not find an answer to the penetrating groundstroke power of a worthy champion. As for what he thought about the Sampras serve, the picture overleaf tells its own story.

One was the average speed of his second serve, but as Sampras still won 61 per cent of points started by his second serve and Becker only 39 per cent, it hardly mattered. Becker also finished 16–8 ahead on volleys but with Sampras building up a 12–4 advantage in passing shots and no less than 16–5 in backhand winners, the figures again reflected his all-round effectiveness.

Becker had plenty of crowd support, not only in the early stages but through to the end when they demanded that he also do a lap of honour in what became the most relaxed and delightfully animated presentation ceremony the Centre Court has ever seen. Becker did not realise at first that the crowd wanted him to follow the champion with a lap of honour. 'I thought they were shouting for Pete to show them the trophy again but he told me, "No, it's you they want." It felt for a moment as if I was the champion.'

In retrospect there seems little doubt that Becker, though clearly fitter than in the previous couple of years, suffered to some extent in the mid-90 degree F temperatures from the mental and physical effort which had gone into his comebacks in the quarter-final against Cedric Pioline and the semi-final against Andre Agassi. The increasing problems he encountered on his serve offered evidence of that. 'I didn't have enough strength and power in my legs that I need to push me into my serves,' he said. In addition to being broken five times, he was also forced to save 11 break points as Sampras steadily elevated his game to an altogether higher level.

Although the double fault which Sampras struck to go 2–3 down in the tie-break gave Becker the impetus to take the first set, it was the double faults which flowed later from the German's racket which were much more significant. There were two when he was broken to trail 1–4 in the second set, another which cost him the third game of the third set and then, most demoralising of all, his 12th and 13th, towards a

total of 15, as he lost the opening game of the fourth set.

Not only that, but while the Becker serve lost its accuracy, as well as its venom, the Sampras serve returned to its winning groove with a vengeance. Indeed there were three aces when he clinched the second set in 27 minutes and three more towards his total of 23 when he held for 3–1 in the fourth. The only time Becker might have forced his way

Consolation for Arantxa Sanchez Vicario as she and Jana Novotna take the women's doubles title from defending champions, Gigi Fernandez and Natasha Zvereva.

Nineteen down – one to go! Martina Navratilova leaps into the arms of fellow American, Jonathan Stark, to celebrate the mixed doubles triumph which took her within one step of equalling Billie Jean King's record of 20 Wimbledon titles.

back into contention was in the tenth game of the third set when Sampras, who had not conceded a point on his four previous service games, went 0–30 as he served for the set, to Becker's defiant backhand pass and one of those lucky net cords which can so easily, in circum-

stances such as this, sow seeds of doubt.

Sampras, however, shrugged them aside, just as he did all other distractions, such as the enormous cheer floating over from Court One when Britain's Martin Lee and James Trotman completed their triumph in the final of the junior boys' doubles.

In the last game, Sampras was caught out of position by a lunging lob from Becker on the first point. There was also a final but forlorn backhand pass from Becker to make it 30–30 – but then came the American's 23rd ace and a Becker forehand which floated meekly into the tramlines.

Sampras's triumph was wholly predictable in form and substance, though on a day when the longest rally was only seven shots, he also revealed the more human touch behind the stern concentration which makes him such a great champion, by throwing not only his shirt and towels into the crowd but also tossing a cup of ice cubes at them.

Just two more matches remained to be decided before the Centre Court would enjoy a well-earned rest until next year. First there was the completion of that women's doubles final halted by fading light at 9.20 the night before. Gigi Fernandez and Natasha Zvereva were seeking their fourth consecutive success – but if anyone deserved a lasting reward for their efforts this year it was surely Sanchez, after her heroic efforts in the singles, and Novotna, who had been runner-up in the ladies' doubles every year since last winning the title with Helena Sukova in 1990.

They resumed, from Sanchez and Novotna's standpoint, at 5–7, 7–5, 4–4 and immediately broke the Fernandez serve when the strength of their returns forced two volleying errors. Sanchez then served out to love before being embraced by Novotna, who also punched the air in delight. It had taken them just four more minutes. 'It's a nice compliment to our professionalism that we could come back and win this title,' said the Spaniard. 'Jana was also down after losing to Steffi

in the semis, but we both had close matches with her and it's no shame to lose to a winner like Steffi.'

There was further disappointment for Fernandez, however, for she and Cyril Suk were then beaten 6–4, 6–4 as Martina Navratilova and Jonathan Stark brought the curtain down on a glorious fortnight with a 6–4, 6–4 victory which, needless to say, was greeted by a cheering, standing ovation. Stark, a former men's doubles champion at the French Open, said he did not need to be asked twice when it was suggested that he might play in the mixed doubles with the former world champion but, because of her television commitments, they did not actually meet until they walked out for their first match together.

When Stark finished the match with an ace it provoked a delighted yell from his partner, who ran over and jumped into his arms and gave him a theatrical kiss at the net. It was, after all, her 19th Wimbledon title and helped compensate for her missing out in the ladies' doubles. Would she return in 1996 to try and equal Billie Jean's record, she was inevitably asked. 'I don't know. I would actually feel a little sad if I did that because I partnered Billie Jean to her 20th title and the only title I've pursued vigorously was my ninth singles win here. But if I do play again next year, I will still be playing to win.'

Court One does not normally attract a particularly large attendance when the men's singles final is taking place next door. This year, though, was an exception, for it was well filled by patriotic souls who relished the sight of an unseeded British pair, Martin Lee, 17, from Worthing, already into the top ten among world junior singles rankings, and James Trotman, also 17, from Suffolk, beating the second seeds, Alejandro Hernandez from Mexico and Marinao Puerto from Argentina, 7–6, 6–4.

The winners, both coached by Ian Barclay at the Rover/LTA School at Bisham Abbey, fought back brilliantly from 1–5 and two breaks down in the

first set, during which they saved two set points before taking it in a 7–2 tie-break. Although they had been together as a pair for more than three years this was their first major success, and it completed a remarkable comeback by Trotman, who could not play for seven months in 1994 because of stress fractures and then contracted glandular fever in Australia within a month of his return.

The record final day attendance which they helped to attract was 22,926, bringing the fortnight's total to 384,882, an increase of 6,909 on 1994. The only sadness, of course, was the absence for the first time that anyone could remember of Fred Perry, who had died during the Australian Open in January. In a touching reference to him during The Champions' Dinner at the Savoy, which has become the traditional final touch to the tournament, John Curry, chairman of The All England Club, pointed out how lucky they had been with the weather, especially as it poured with rain for most of the middle Sunday, when everyone takes a day off. 'I'm sure this year we had Fred watching over us,' he said.

Above: Martin Lee and James Trotman soak up the pressures of a Wimbledon final and an extremely hot day before James can celebrate their win in front of the excited and patriotic crowd.

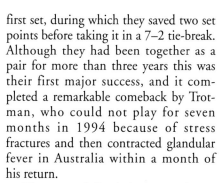

Fred Perry would have appreciated the quality of play shown by this year's singles champions, Steffi Graf and Pete Sampras.

The Ladies' Doubles Championship
Jana Novotna and Arantxa Sanchez Vicario

The Ladies' Singles Championship
Steffi Graf

The Mixed Doubles Championship
Jonathan Stark and Martina Navratilova

The 35 and over Gentlemen's Invitation Doubles
Leif Shiras and Peter McNamara

The 35 and over Ladies' Invitation Doubles
Wendy Turnbull and Virginia Wade

The 45 and over Gentlemen's Invitation Doubles
John Newcombe and Tony Roche

The Gentlemen's Singles Championship
Pete Sampras

The Gentlemen's Doubles Championship
Todd Woodbridge and Mark Woodforde

The Boys' Doubles Championship
Martin Lee and James Trotman

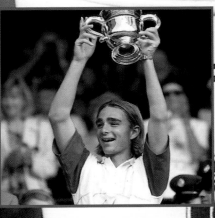

The Boys' Singles Championship
Olivier Mutis

The Girls' Doubles Championship
Cara Black and Aleksandra Olsza

The Girls' Singles Championship
Aleksandra Olsza

CHAMPIONSHIP RECORDS

1995

LADIES

- **86** Adams Miss K.M. *(USA)*
- Amiach Miss S. *(France)*
- **63** Appelmans Miss S. *(Belgium)*
- **72** Arendt Miss N.J. *(USA)*
- **110** Avila Miss N. *(Spain)*
- **62** Babel Miss M.B. *(Germany)*
- Barclay Miss C.G. *(Australia)*
- Basting Miss Y. *(Netherlands)*
- **101** Basuki Miss Y. *(Indonesia)*
- **125** Baudone Miss N. *(Italy)*
- **45** Begerow Miss P. *(Germany)*
- Bernard Miss M. *(Canada)*
- **111** Bobkova Miss R. *(Czech Republic)*
- Bollegraf Miss M.M. *(Netherlands)*
- Bond Miss E.L. *(Great Britain)*
- **6** Boogert Miss K. *(Netherlands)*
- **41** Bradtke Mrs N. *(Australia)*
- **85** Cacic Miss S. *(USA)*
- Callens Miss E.S.H. *(Belgium)*
- **95** Carlsson Miss A. *(Sweden)*
- **50** Cecchini Miss A-M. *(Italy)*
- **4** Coetzer Miss A.J. *(South Africa)*
- **107** Courtois Miss L. *(Belgium)*
- **93** Cross Miss K.M. *(Great Britain)*
- Dahlman Miss N. *(Finland)*
- **64** Date Miss K. *(Japan)*
- **32** Davenport Miss L.A. *(USA)*
- **53** de Swardt Miss M. *(South Africa)*
- **36** Dechaume-Balleret Mrs A. *(France)*
- Delisle Miss C. *(Canada)*
- **55** Demongeot Miss I. *(France)*
- **98** Dopfer Miss S. *(Austria)*
- **23** Dragomir Miss R. *(Romania)*
- Driehuis Miss I. *(Netherlands)*
- **35** Durie Miss J.M. *(Great Britain)*
- **126** Endo Miss M. *(Japan)*
- **68** Farina Miss S. *(Italy)*
- **71** Feber Miss N. *(Belgium)*
- **70** Fendick Miss P.A. *(USA)*
- **31** Fernandez Miss G. *(USA)*
- **17** Fernandez Miss M.J. *(USA)*
- **117** Frankl Miss S. *(Germany)*
- **80** Frazier Miss A. *(USA)*
- **20** Fusai Miss A. *(France)*
- **122** Garrison-Jackson Mrs Z.L. *(USA)*
- Garrone Miss L. *(Italy)*
- **47** Gavaldon Miss A. *(Mexico)*
- **66** Ghirardi Miss L. *(France)*
- Godridge Miss K. *(Australia)*
- **54** Golarsa Miss L. *(Italy)*
- **11** Gorrochategui Miss I. *(Argentina)*
- **1** Graf Miss S. *(Germany)*
- **103** Graham Miss D.A. *(USA)*
- Grande Miss R. *(Italy)*
- **57** Grossman Miss A. *(USA)*
- Guse Miss K-A. *(Australia)*
- **18** Habsudova Miss K. *(Slovakia)*
- **43** Halard Miss J. *(France)*
- **75** Harvey-Wild Miss L.M. *(USA)*
- Hetherington Miss J.M. *(Canada)*
- **2** Hingis Miss M. *(Switzerland)*
- Hiraki Miss R. *(Japan)*
- Horn Miss L. *(South Africa)*
- **113** Huber Miss A. *(Germany)*
- **118** Hy-Boulais Mrs P. *(Canada)*
- **10** Ignatieva Miss T. *(Belarus)*
- **27** Jelfs Miss E.E. *(Great Britain)*
- Jensen Miss R. *(USA)*
- **52** Kamio Miss Y. *(Japan)*
- **88** Kamstra Miss P. *(Netherlands)*
- **94** Kandarr Miss J. *(Germany)*
- **58** Keller Miss A.A. *(USA)*
- **124** Kochta Miss M. *(Germany)*
- Koutstaal Miss M. *(Netherlands)*
- **114** Krizan Miss T. *(Slovenia)*
- **78** Kruger Miss J. *(South Africa)*
- **34** Kschwendt Miss K. *(Germany)*
- **30** Labat Miss F. *(Argentina)*
- Lake Miss V. *(Great Britain)*
- Langrova Miss P. *(Czech Republic)*
- **13** Lee Miss L. *(USA)*
- **67** Likhovtseva Miss E. *(Russia)*
- Lindstrom Miss M. *(Sweden)*
- Lugina Miss O. *(Ukraine)*
- **48** Majoli Miss I. *(Croatia)*
- **7** Makarova Miss E. *(Russia)*
- **22** Maleeva Miss K. *(Bulgaria)*
- Maniokova Miss E. *(Russia)*
- **92** Martinek Miss V. *(Germany)*
- **96** Martinez Miss C. *(Spain)*
- **108** McGrath Miss M.J. *(USA)*
- **82** McNeil Miss L.M. *(USA)*
- **76** McQuillan Miss R. *(Australia)*
- **102** Medvedeva Miss N. *(Ukraine)*
- **83** Meier Miss S. *(Germany)*
- Melicharova Miss E. *(Czech Republic)*
- **15** Miller Miss M. *(Great Britain)*
- **40** Miyagi Miss N. *(Japan)*
- **69** Monami Miss D. *(Belgium)*
- Moore Miss J. *(Great Britain)*
- Muns-Jagerman Mrs N.A.M. *(Netherlands)*
- Nagano Miss H. *(Japan)*
- **104** Nagatsuka Miss K. *(Japan)*
- Nagelsen Miss B. *(USA)*
- Navratilova Miss M. *(USA)*
- **109** Neiland Mrs L. *(Latvia)*
- **44** Nejedly Miss J. *(Canada)*
- **46** Nideffer Mrs R. *(South Africa)*
- **33** Novotna Miss J. *(Czech Republic)*
- **24** Oremans Miss M. *(Netherlands)*
- **19** Park Miss S-H. *(South Korea)*
- **26** Paulus Miss B. *(Austria)*
- Paz Miss M. *(Argentina)*
- **61** Perfetti Miss F. *(Italy)*
- **97** Pierce Miss M. *(France)*
- **87** Pitkowski Miss S. *(France)*
- **90** Pizzichini Miss G. *(Italy)*
- Pleming Miss L. *(Australia)*
- **60** Po Miss K. *(USA)*
- Poruri Miss L. *(USA)*
- **37** Porwik Miss C. *(Germany)*
- **12** Probst Miss W. *(Germany)*
- **74** Pullin Miss J.M. *(Great Britain)*
- **25** Radford Miss K. *(Australia)*
- **73** Raymond Miss L.M. *(USA)*
- **123** Reinach Miss E. *(South Africa)*
- **115** Reinstadler Miss B. *(Austria)*
- **119** Richterova Miss L. *(Czech Republic)*
- **79** Rottier Miss S. *(Netherlands)*
- **5** Ruano Pascual Miss V. *(Spain)*
- **120** Rubin Miss C. *(USA)*
- **65** Sabatini Miss G. *(Argentina)*
- **128** Sanchez Vicario Miss A. *(Spain)*
- **81** Sawamatsu Miss N. *(Japan)*
- **21** Schnell Miss M. *(Austria)*
- **112** Schultz-McCarthy Mrs B. *(Netherlands)*
- **3** Schwarz-Ritter Mrs P. *(Austria)*
- Scott Miss D. *(USA)*
- Sharpe Miss K. *(Australia)*
- **14** Shriver Miss P.H. *(USA)*
- **29** Siddall Miss S-A. *(Great Britain)*
- Simpson Miss R. *(Canada)*
- **28** Singer Miss C. *(Germany)*
- **105** Smashnova Miss A. *(Israel)*
- **77** Spirlea Miss I. *(Romania)*
- **91** Stafford Miss S.C. *(USA)*
- **84** Strandlund Miss M. *(Sweden)*
- **9** Stubbs Miss R.P. *(Australia)*
- **127** Studenikova Miss K. *(Slovakia)*
- **116** Sugiyama Miss A. *(Japan)*
- **49** Sukova Miss H. *(Czech Republic)*
- Tarabini Miss P. *(Argentina)*
- **99** Tauziat Miss N. *(France)*
- **89** Temesvari Miss A. *(Hungary)*
- **39** Testud Miss S. *(France)*
- Tu Miss M. *(USA)*
- Van Lottum Miss N. *(France)*
- **100** Vento Miss M. *(Venezuela)*
- Vildova Miss H. *(Czech Republic)*
- Vis Miss C.M. *(Netherlands)*
- **42** Wagner Mrs E. *(Germany)*
- **121** Wainwright Miss A.M.H. *(Great Britain)*
- **51** Watanabe Miss J. *(USA)*
- **8** Werdel Witmeyer Mrs M. *(USA)*
- White Miss R.M. *(USA)*
- **59** Whitlinger-Jones Mrs T.S. *(USA)*
- **38** Wiesner Mrs J.K. *(Austria)*
- **56** Wood Miss C.J. *(Great Britain)*
- Woodroffe Miss L.A. *(Great Britain)*
- **106** Zrubakova Miss R. *(Slovakia)*
- **16** Zvereva Miss N. *(Belarus)*

GENTLEMEN

- Adams D. *(South Africa)*
- **1** Agassi A. *(USA)*
- Albano P. *(Argentina)*
- **34** Alvarez E. *(Spain)*
- Antonitsch A. *(Austria)*
- **35** Apell J. *(Sweden)*
- Arnold P. *(Argentina)*
- Arthurs W. *(Australia)*
- Bale L.J. *(South Africa)*
- Barnard M. *(South Africa)*
- **42** Barthez L. *(France)*
- **88** Bates M.J. *(Great Britain)*
- Bauer M. *(USA)*
- **54** Baur P. *(Germany)*
- **33** Becker B. *(Germany)*
- Bergh R. *(Sweden)*
- **73** Bergstrom C. *(Sweden)*
- **30** Bjorkman J. *(Sweden)*
- **8** Black B. *(Zimbabwe)*
- **89** Boetsch A. *(France)*
- **53** Borwick N. *(Australia)*
- **127** Braasch K. *(Germany)*
- Brandi C. *(Italy)*
- Broad N. *(Great Britain)*
- **29** Burgsmuller L. *(Germany)*
- **110** Burillo J. *(Spain)*
- **56** Caratti C. *(Italy)*
- **77** Carbonell T. *(Spain)*
- **9** Carlsen K. *(Denmark)*
- **45** Cash P. *(Australia)*
- **91** Chang A. *(Canada)*
- **64** Chang M. *(USA)*
- **38** Chesnokov A. *(Russia)*
- Conde J.A. *(Spain)*
- Connell G. *(Canada)*
- **49** Courier J. *(USA)*
- **7** Cowan B. *(Great Britain)*
- Davids H.J. *(Netherlands)*
- Davis S.E. *(USA)*
- De Jager J-L. *(South Africa)*
- **117** Delaitre O. *(France)*
- Delgado J. *(Great Britain)*
- **66** Dewulf F. *(Belgium)*
- **39** Dosedel S. *(Czech Republic)*
- Doyle G. *(Australia)*
- **121** Draper S. *(Australia)*
- **108** Dreekmann H. *(Germany)*
- Eagle J. *(Australia)*
- **48** Edberg S. *(Sweden)*
- **18** Eltingh J. *(Netherlands)*
- **97** Enqvist T. *(Sweden)*
- **119** Erlich E. *(Israel)*
- Ferreira E. *(South Africa)*
- **32** Ferreira W. *(South Africa)*
- **123** Fetterlein F. *(Denmark)*
- Fitzgerald J.B. *(Australia)*
- Flach D. *(USA)*
- **50** Flach K. *(USA)*
- Flegl V. *(Czech Republic)*
- Florent A. *(Australia)*
- **113** Forget G. *(France)*
- Foster A.L. *(Great Britain)*
- **99** Frana J. *(Argentina)*
- **106** Furlan R. *(Italy)*
- Galbraith P. *(USA)*
- **60** Gaudenzi A. *(Italy)*
- **69** Gloria L. *(USA)*
- **22** Goellner M. *(Germany)*
- Grabb J. *(USA)*
- **26** Haarhuis P. *(Netherlands)*
- Hand P.T. *(Great Britain)*
- Haygarth B. *(South Africa)*
- **114** Henderson G. *(Great Britain)*
- **125** Henman T. *(Great Britain)*
- **68** Hlasek J. *(Switzerland)*
- **92** Ho T. *(USA)*
- Holm H. *(Sweden)*
- Ireland J. *(Australia)*
- **96** Ivanisevic G. *(Croatia)*
- **98** Jarryd A. *(Sweden)*
- Jensen L.B. *(USA)*
- Jensen M. *(USA)*
- Johnson D. *(USA)*
- Jones K. *(USA)*
- **86** Jonsson L. *(Sweden)*
- **111** Joyce M. *(USA)*
- **65** Kafelnikov Y. *(Russia)*
- **67** Karbacher B. *(Germany)*
- Kempers T. *(Netherlands)*
- Kilderry P. *(Australia)*
- Kinnear K. *(USA)*
- **104** Knowles M. *(Bahamas)*
- **62** Korda P. *(Czech Republic)*
- **80** Krajicek R. *(Netherlands)*
- Kratzmann A. *(Australia)*
- **74** Krickstein A. *(USA)*
- Kristiansson O. *(Sweden)*
- Kronemann T. *(USA)*
- **40** Kroslak J. *(Slovakia)*
- **76** Kucera K. *(Slovakia)*
- **95** Lareau S. *(Canada)*
- Larkham T. *(Australia)*
- Lavalle L. *(Mexico)*
- Leach R. *(USA)*
- **100** Leconte H. *(France)*
- **52** Lopez-Moron A. *(Spain)*
- Lozano J. *(Mexico)*
- Lucena M. *(USA)*
- **105** Maclagan C.M. *(Great Britain)*
- Macpherson D. *(Australia)*
- MacPhie B. *(USA)*
- **90** Marques N. *(Portugal)*
- **81** Martin T. *(USA)*
- **47** Martinez O. *(Spain)*
- **78** Masur W. *(Australia)*
- **6** Matheson R. *(Great Britain)*
- **101** Matsuoka S. *(Japan)*
- **4** McEnroe P. *(USA)*
- **16** Medvedev A. *(Ukraine)*
- Melville S. *(USA)*
- Middleton T.J. *(USA)*
- Montana F. *(USA)*
- **36** Morgan J. *(Australia)*
- **11** Mronz A. *(Germany)*
- Muller G. *(South Africa)*
- **61** Nargiso D. *(Italy)*
- **83** Nestor D. *(Canada)*
- Nijssen T. *(Netherlands)*
- **46** Norman D. *(Belgium)*
- Norval P. *(South Africa)*
- **14** Noszaly S. *(Hungary)*
- Noteboom S. *(Netherlands)*
- **102** Novacek K. *(Czech Republic)*
- Nyborg P. *(Sweden)*
- **118** O'Brien A. *(USA)*
- **20** Olhovskiy A. *(Russia)*
- **75** Ondruska M. *(South Africa)*
- Oosting M. *(Netherlands)*
- **2** Painter A. *(Australia)*
- **122** Palmer J. *(USA)*
- Pate D. *(USA)*
- **82** Pereira N. *(Venezuela)*
- **23** Petchey M.R.J. *(Great Britain)*
- Philippoussis M. *(Australia)*
- Pimek L. *(Belgium)*
- **51** Pioline C. *(France)*
- **41** Pozzi G. *(Italy)*
- **21** Prinosil D. *(Germany)*
- **27** Rafter P. *(Australia)*
- Randall D. *(USA)*
- **55** Raoux G. *(France)*
- **3** Reneberg R.A. *(USA)*
- **70** Renzenbrink J. *(Germany)*
- Richardson A.L. *(Great Britain)*
- Riglewski U. *(Germany)*
- **103** Rios M. *(Chile)*
- Roig F. *(Spain)*
- **112** Rosset M. *(Switzerland)*
- **87** Rostagno D. *(USA)*
- **63** Roux L. *(France)*
- **115** Rusedski G. *(Great Britain)*
- **15** Ruud C. *(Norway)*
- **128** Sampras P. *(USA)*
- **19** Santoro F. *(France)*
- **84** Sapsford D.E. *(Great Britain)*
- **12** Schalken S. *(Netherlands)*
- Seguso R. *(USA)*
- **79** Shelton B. *(USA)*
- **37** Siemerink J. *(Netherlands)*
- **116** Simian S. *(France)*
- **124** Sinner M. *(Germany)*
- **25** Spadea V. *(USA)*
- **93** Stark J. *(USA)*
- **58** Steven B. *(New Zealand)*
- **17** Stich M. *(Germany)*
- **109** Stolle S. *(Australia)*
- **59** Stoltenberg J. *(Australia)*
- Suk C. *(Czech Republic)*
- **13** Tarango J. *(USA)*
- **85** Tebbutt M. *(Australia)*
- **120** Thoms A. *(Germany)*
- Thorne K. *(USA)*
- **44** Tramacchi P. *(Australia)*
- **10** Ulihrach B. *(Czech Republic)*
- Ullyett K. *(South Africa)*
- **31** Vacek D. *(Czech Republic)*
- Van Emburgh G. *(USA)*
- **94** Vasek R. *(Czech Republic)*
- Visser D.T. *(South Africa)*
- **72** Volkov A. *(Russia)*
- Wahlgren L-A. *(Sweden)*
- Waite J. *(USA)*
- **71** Washington M. *(USA)*
- **126** Wekesa P. *(Kenya)*
- **5** Wheaton D. *(USA)*
- Wibier F. *(Netherlands)*
- **24** Wilander M. *(Sweden)*
- **107** Wilkinson C. *(Great Britain)*
- Winnink J. *(Netherlands)*
- **43** Woodbridge T.A. *(Australia)*
- **28** Woodforde M. *(Australia)*
- **57** Zoecke M. *(Germany)*

GIRLS

- Andriyani Miss L. *(Indonesia)*
- Austin Miss L. *(Great Britain)*
- **2** Barabanschikova Miss O. *(Belarus)*
- **18** Basica Miss A. *(USA)*
- **1** Basting Miss Y. *(Netherlands)*
- **12** Black Miss C. *(Zimbabwe)*
- Blackburn Miss T. *(Great Britain)*
- Callow Miss T. *(Great Britain)*
- **47** Canepa Miss A. *(Italy)*
- **14** Castera Miss A. *(France)*
- **37** Cervanova Miss L. *(Slovakia)*
- **58** Chan Miss W.L. *(Hong Kong)*
- **7** Chiew Miss E. *(Malaysia)*
- **9** Chladkova Miss D. *(Czech Republic)*
- Choudhury Miss J. *(Great Britain)*
- **49** Cocheteux Miss A. *(France)*
- **25** D'Agostini Miss M. *(Brazil)*
- **10** De Beer Miss S. *(South Africa)*
- **27** Dechy Miss N. *(France)*
- **6** Del Valle Prieto Miss M. *(Mexico)*
- **16** Drake Brockman Miss S.E. *(Australia)*
- **48** Ellwood Miss A. *(Australia)*
- Fletcher Miss L. *(Great Britain)*
- **15** Gaviria Miss D. *(Peru)*
- **20** Goldstein Miss K. *(Mexico)*
- **51** Halsell Miss S. *(USA)*
- Hearn Miss F. *(Great Britain)*
- **63** Hermida Miss P. *(Spain)*
- **3** Inoue Miss H. *(Japan)*
- **56** Jeon Miss M-R. *(Korea)*
- **44** Khoo Miss C-B. *(Malaysia)*
- **46** Klosel Miss S. *(Germany)*
- **64** Kournikova Miss A. *(Russia)*
- **5** Lishman Miss F.E. *(Great Britain)*
- **19** Mandula Miss P. *(Hungary)*
- Madden Miss C. *(South Africa)*
- **59** Marosi Miss K. *(Hungary)*
- **38** Mauresmo Miss A. *(France)*
- **36** Mellis Miss Z. *(Great Britain)*
- **54** Miller Miss M. *(Great Britain)*
- **43** Monhartova Miss A. *(Czech Republic)*
- **35** Morariu Miss C. *(USA)*
- **60** Musgrave Miss T. *(Australia)*
- **23** Nacuk Miss S. *(Yugoslavia)*
- **40** Nagy Miss K. *(Hungary)*
- **42** Obata Miss S. *(Japan)*
- Ogan Miss L. *(Great Britain)*
- **24** Olsza Miss A. *(Poland)*
- Osman Miss J. *(Great Britain)*
- **8** Osterloh Miss L. *(USA)*
- **52** Palme Miss K. *(Mexico)*
- **21** Pastikova Miss M. *(Czech Republic)*
- **61** Pirsu Miss A. *(Romania)*
- **26** Plivelitsch Miss T. *(Germany)*
- **50** Poutchek Miss T. *(Belarus)*
- **34** Prakusya Miss W. *(Indonesia)*
- **62** Radeljevic Miss A. *(Croatia)*
- **30** Reeves Miss S. *(USA)*
- Richardson Miss J. *(Australia)*
- **39** Rojas Miss M.E. *(Peru)*
- **22** Roubanova Miss E. *(Great Britain)*
- **4** Sandu Miss R. *(Romania)*
- **53** Schnyder Miss P. *(Switzerland)*
- **57** Schonfeldova Miss J. *(Czech Republic)*
- **41** Schwartz Miss B. *(Austria)*
- **28** Sfar Miss S. *(Tunisia)*
- **55** Steck Miss J. *(South Africa)*
- **32** Swart Miss G. *(South Africa)*
- **33** Tanasugarn Miss T. *(Thailand)*
- **45** Tordoff Miss A. *(Great Britain)*
- **17** Varmuzova Miss L. *(San Marino)*
- **13** Vavrinec Miss M. *(Switzerland)*
- **29** Venkatesan Miss A. *(Australia)*
- **11** Weingartner Miss M. *(Germany)*
- **31** Weng Miss T. *(Taipeh)*

BOYS

- **43** Aybar A. *(Dominican Republic)*
- **40** Bachelot J-F. *(France)*
- **3** Bardoczky K. *(Hungary)*
- **8** Borgula B. *(Slovakia)*
- **29** Bracciali D. *(Italy)*
- **36** Brandt J-R. *(Germany)*
- **5** Cadart R. *(France)*
- **16** Canas G. *(Argentina)*
- **11** Cardozo F. *(Argentina)*
- **46** Cerdera R. *(Argentina)*
- **62** Chadha V. *(India)*
- **18** Clarke S. *(Great Britain)*
- **15** Coetzee J. *(South Africa)*
- **57** De Melo D. *(Brazil)*
- **48** Delgado J. *(Great Britain)*
- **64** Erlich E. *(Israel)*
- **58** Gimelstob J. *(USA)*
- **24** Haas T. *(Germany)*
- **10** Hadad A. *(Israel)*
- **38** Haran B. *(Great Britain)*
- **39** Hemeda H. *(Egypt)*
- **17** Hernandez A. *(Mexico)*
- Hill G. *(USA)*
- **37** Hui J. *(Hong Kong)*
- **35** Ishii Y. *(Japan)*
- **20** Jancso M. *(Hungary)*
- **9** Jonsson F. *(Sweden)*
- **1** Kiefer N. *(Germany)*
- **6** Kim D-H. *(South Korea)*
- **14** Kobzos P. *(Switzerland)*
- **45** Krajan Z. *(Croatia)*
- **41** Kratochvil M. *(Switzerland)*
- **33** Lee J-M. *(South Korea)*
- **25** Lee M. *(Great Britain)*
- **21** Levy H. *(Israel)*
- **47** Matijasevic D. *(Yugoslavia)*
- **26** Moldovan I. *(Romania)*
- **53** Mutis O. *(France)*
- **63** Nash N. *(Australia)*
- **13** Orellana K. *(Venezuela)*
- **12** Osterrieth A. *(Great Britain)*
- **27** Perlant J.B. *(France)*
- **32** Puerta M. *(Argentina)*
- **34** Rehnqvist B.C. *(Sweden)*
- **44** Ribeiro R. *(Brazil)*
- **55** Robichaud J. *(Canada)*
- **52** Romero Y. *(Venezuela)*
- **51** Russell M. *(USA)*
- **23** Saurav P. *(India)*
- **22** Schlachter R. *(Brazil)*
- **50** Sciortino D. *(Italy)*
- **49** Seetzen U-J. *(Germany)*
- **7** Sidia S. *(Tunisia)*
- **42** Stepanek R. *(Czech Republic)*
- **31** Susnjak T. *(New Zealand)*
- **56** Tabara M. *(Czech Republic)*
- **54** Timfjord N.R.D. *(Sweden)*
- **60** Trotman J.M. *(Great Britain)*
- **4** Vanek J. *(Czech Republic)*
- **59** Voltchkov V. *(Belarus)*
- **30** Wessels P. *(Netherlands)*
- **2** Witoonpanich B. *(Thailand)*
- Woolley M. *(Great Britain)*
- **19** Wolters R. *(USA)*
- **61** Zahirovic M. *(Bosnia-Herzegovina)*

Bold figures denote position in Singles Draw

The winner will become the holder, for the year only, of the CHALLENGE CUP presented by The All England Lawn Tennis and Croquet Club. The winner will receive a silver replica of the Challenge Cup. A silver salver will be presented to the runner-up and a bronze medal to each defeated semi-finalist.

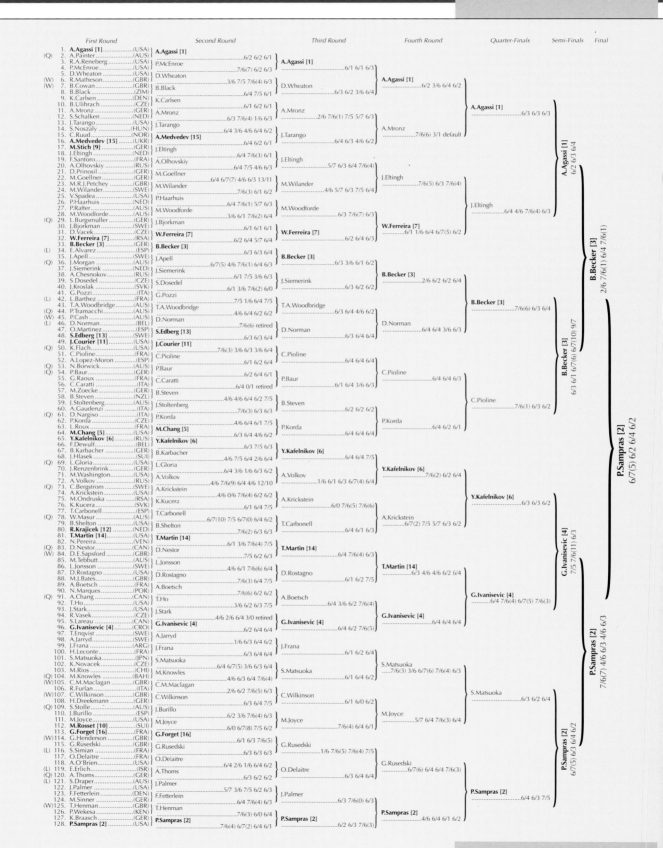

Heavy type denotes seeded players. The encircled figure against names denotes the order in which they have been seeded.
(W) = Wild card. (Q) = Qualifier. (L) = Lucky loser.
The matches are the best of five sets

THE GENTLEMEN'S DOUBLES CHAMPIONSHIP

Holders: T. A. Woodbridge and M. Woodforde

The winners become the holders, for one year only, of the CHALLENGE CUPS presented by the OXFORD UNIVERSITY LAWN TENNIS CLUB and the late SIR HERBERT WILBERFORCE respectively. The winners also receive silver replicas of the Challenge Cups. A silver salver is presented to each of the runners-up, and a bronze medal to each defeated semi-finalist.

	First Round	Second Round	Third Round	Quarter-Finals	Semi-Finals	Final

First Round

1. J.Eltingh (NED) & P.Haarhuis (NED) .... [1]
(W) 2. M.R.J.Petchey (GBR) & C.Wilkinson (GBR)
3. M.Sinner (GER) & J.Winnink (NED)
4. M.Bauer (USA) & J.Ireland (AUS)
5. J.A.Conde (ESP) & N.Marques (POR)
6. P.Nyborg (SWE) & K.Ullyett (RSA)
(Q) 7. J.Delgado (GBR) & G.Henderson (GBR)
8. L.J.Bale (RSA) & J-L.De Jager (RSA) .... [15]
9. T.Ho (USA) & B.Steven (NZL) .... [9]
10. D.Norman (BEL) & L.Pimek (BEL)
11. C.Brandi (ITA) & M.Ondruska (RSA)
12. A.Mronz (GER) & U.Riglewski (GER)
13. J.Eagle (AUS) & A.Florent (AUS)
14. P.Albano (ARG) & H.J.Davids (NED)
15. R.Leach (USA) & S.Melville (USA)
16. C.Suk (CZE) & D.Vacek (CZE) .... [8]
17. B.Black (ZIM) & J.Stark (USA) .... [4]
18. D.Adams (RSA) & T.Nijssen (NED)
19. S.Lareau (CAN) & B.MacPhie (USA)
(Q) 20. D.Flach (USA) & M.Joyce (USA)
21. S.Noteboom (NED) & F.Wibier (NED)
22. L.B.Jensen (USA) & M.Jensen (USA)
23. A.Kratzmann (AUS) & P.Wekesa (KEN)
24. M.Goellner (GER) & Y.Kafelnikov (RUS) .... [14]
25. A.Olhovskiy (RUS) & J.Siemerink (NED) .... [12]
26. D.Randall (AUS) & G.Van Emburgh (USA)
27. A.L.Foster (GBR) & D.E.Sapsford (GBR)
28. T.Kempers (NED) & P.Kilderry (AUS)
29. W.Arthurs (AUS) & N.Broad (GBR)
(W) 30. B.Cowan (GBR) & A.L.Richardson (GBR)
31. T.Carbonell (ESP) & F.Roig (ESP)
32. J.Palmer (USA) & R.A.Reneberg (USA) .... [6]
33. J.Grabb (USA) & P.McEnroe (USA) .... [5]
(Q) 34. S.Draper (AUS) & P.Tramacchi (AUS)
35. D.Johnson (USA) & K.Thorne (USA)
36. O.Delaitre (FRA) & D.Prinosil (GER)
37. K.Jones (USA) & D.Pate (USA)
38. J.B.Fitzgerald (AUS) & A.Jarryd (SWE)
39. L.Lavalle (MEX) & F.Montana (USA)
40. M.Knowles (BAH) & D.Nestor (CAN) .... [11]
41. A.O'Brien (USA) & S.Stolle (AUS) .... [13]
42. M.Barnard (RSA) & E.Ferreira (RSA)
43. D.Nargiso (ITA) & G.Raoux (FRA)
44. K.Novacek (CZE) & M.Wilander (SWE)
45. J.Frana (ARG) & G.Muller (RSA)
46. S.E.Davis (USA) & M.Lucena (USA)
47. G.Forget (FRA) & J.Hlasek (SUI)
48. G.Connell (CAN) & P.Galbraith (USA) .... [3]
49. J.Apell (SWE) & J.Bjorkman (SWE) .... [7]
50. B.Haygarth (RSA) & D.T.Visser (RSA)
51. A.Antonitsch (AUT) & K.Kinnear (USA)
52. O.Kristiansson (SWE) & L-A.Wahlgren (SWE)
53. R.Bergh (SWE) & J.Waite (USA)
54. M.Philippoussis (AUS) & P.Rafter (AUS)
55. P.Arnold (ARG) & J.Lozano (MEX)
56. T.Kronemann (USA) & D.Macpherson (AUS) .... [10]
57. P.Norval (RSA) & M.Oosting (NED) .... [16]
58. G.Doyle (AUS) & T.Larkham (AUS)
(L) 59. V.Flegl (CZE) & B.Shelton (USA)
(W) 60. P.T.Hand (GBR) & R.Matheson (GBR)
61. H.Holm (SWE) & J.Tarango (USA)
(W) 62. M.J.Bates (GBR) & T.Henman (GBR)
(W) 63. K.Flach (USA) & R.Seguso (USA)
64. T.A.Woodbridge (AUS) & M.Woodforde (AUS) .... [2]

Second Round

J.Eltingh (NED) & P.Haarhuis (NED) [1]
6/3 6/4 6/4

M.Bauer (USA) & J.Ireland (AUS)
7/5 7/6(8) 6/2

J.A.Conde (ESP) & N.Marques (POR)
7/6(2) 7/6(5) 7/5

L.J.Bale (RSA) & J-L.De Jager (RSA) [15]
6/4 6/4 6/(7)

T.Ho (USA) & B.Steven (NZL) [9]
6/(7) 4/5 6/2 6/2

C.Brandi (ITA) & M.Ondruska (RSA)
5/7 5/7 7/6(4) 7/6(1) 6/2

J.Eagle (AUS) & A.Florent (AUS)
7/6(2) 4/6 4/6 6/4 7/5

R.Leach (USA) & S.Melville (USA)
6/3 6/3 6/3

B.Black (ZIM) & J.Stark (USA) [4]
6/1 6/4 6/1

S.Lareau (CAN) & B.MacPhie (USA)
6/3 6/2 6/4

S.Noteboom (NED) & F.Wibier (NED)
7/6(1) 5/7 6/3 6/4

M.Goellner (GER) & Y.Kafelnikov (RUS) [14]
6/4 6/4 6/4

A.Olhovskiy (RUS) & J.Siemerink (NED) [12]

T.Kempers (NED) & P.Kilderry (AUS)
6/2 7/6(1) 6/3

B.Cowan (GBR) & A.L.Richardson (GBR)
7/6(0) 3/6 6/3 6/3

J.Palmer (USA) & R.A.Reneberg (USA) [6]
7/6(4) 3/6 3/6 6/4 6/3

S.Draper (AUS) & P.Tramacchi (AUS)
6/4 6/4 1/6 7/5

O.Delaitre (FRA) & D.Prinosil (GER)
6/3 6/4

K.Jones (USA) & D.Pate (USA)
0/6 2/6 7/6(5) 7/6(7) 12/10

M.Knowles (BAH) & D.Nestor (CAN) [11]
7/6(2)

A.O'Brien (USA) & S.Stolle (AUS) [13]
2/6 7/5 6/3 6/4

D.Nargiso (ITA) & G.Raoux (FRA)
7/6(6)

S.E.Davis (USA) & M.Lucena (USA)
6/2 6/7(4) 3/6 6/3 15/13

G.Forget (FRA) & J.Hlasek (SUI)
6/3 6/1 7/6(3) 6/3

J.Apell (SWE) & J.Bjorkman (SWE) [7]
7/6(3) 7/6(7) 6/4

A.Antonitsch (AUT) & K.Kinnear (USA)

M.Philippoussis (AUS) & P.Rafter (AUS)

T.Kronemann (USA) & D.Macpherson (AUS) [10]
6/7(7) 6/3 6/7(8) 6/3 7/5

P.Norval (RSA) & M.Oosting (NED) [16]
6/0 2/6 6/3 6/2

P.T.Hand (GBR) & R.Matheson (GBR)
4/6 6/3 3/6 7/6(3) 6/3

H.Holm (SWE) & J.Tarango (USA)
7/6(5) 5/7 6/4 7/5

T.A.Woodbridge (AUS) & M.Woodforde (AUS) [2]
6/4 6/0 7/5

Third Round

J.Eltingh (NED) & P.Haarhuis (NED) [1]
6/3 6/2 6/2

L.J.Bale (RSA) & J-L.De Jager (RSA) [15]
4/6 6/4 4/6 6/4 6/2

C.Brandi (ITA) & M.Ondruska (RSA)
0/0 0-15 retired

R.Leach (USA) & S.Melville (USA)
6/3 6/3 6/3

B.Black (ZIM) & J.Stark (USA) [4]
4/6 6/3 6/3 7/5

M.Goellner (GER) & Y.Kafelnikov (RUS) [14]
6/1 6/4 7/5

A.Olhovskiy (RUS) & J.Siemerink (NED) [12]
6/4 7/5 4/6 7/6(1)

J.Palmer (USA) & R.A.Reneberg (USA) [6]
6/3 6/4 1/6 7/5

O.Delaitre (FRA) & D.Prinosil (GER)
7/6(6) 2/6 6/7(3) 7/6(0) 6/0

M.Knowles (BAH) & D.Nestor (CAN) [11]
6/4 7/6(5) 6/3

A.O'Brien (USA) & S.Stolle (AUS) [13]
7/6(6) 6/3 6/4

G.Forget (FRA) & J.Hlasek (SUI)
7/6(0) 6/4

J.Apell (SWE) & J.Bjorkman (SWE) [7]
7/6(3) 7/6(5) 6/3

M.Philippoussis (AUS) & P.Rafter (AUS)
5/7 7/6 4/4 6/2 6/4

T.A.Woodbridge (AUS) & M.Woodforde (AUS) [2]
6/4 6/1 6/4

Quarter-Finals

J.Eltingh (NED) & P.Haarhuis (NED) [1]
6/3 6/2 3/6 6/3

R.Leach (USA) & S.Melville (USA)
6/3 7/6(3) 6/1

M.Goellner (GER) & Y.Kafelnikov (RUS) [14]
7/6(4) 7/6(3) 7/6(6)

A.Olhovskiy (RUS) & J.Siemerink (NED) [12]
7/6(2) 7/5 6/7(5) 6/3

M.Knowles (BAH) & D.Nestor (CAN) [11]
6/2 6/2 6/2

G.Forget (FRA) & J.Hlasek (SUI)
2/6 7/6(2) 7/6(3) 7/6(3)

M.Philippoussis (AUS) & P.Rafter (AUS)
6/3 6/4 6/4

T.A.Woodbridge (AUS) & M.Woodforde (AUS) [2]
6/3 7/6(7) 6/3

Semi-Finals

R.Leach (USA) & S.Melville (USA)
6/4 6/4 3/6 7/6(5)

M.Goellner (GER) & Y.Kafelnikov (RUS) [14]
7/6(5) 6/7(3) 6/3 6/4

M.Knowles (BAH) & D.Nestor (CAN) [11]
6/3 6/4 6/3

T.A.Woodbridge (AUS) & M.Woodforde (AUS) [2]
6/2 1/6 6/2 7/6(7)

Final

R.Leach (USA) & S.Melville (USA)
3/6 7/6(12) 6/7(2) 7/6(3) 6/3

T.A.Woodbridge (AUS) & M.Woodforde (AUS) [2]
7/5 7/6(8) 7/6(5)

Heavy type denotes seeded players.
The encircled figure against names denotes the order in which they have been seeded.
(W) = Wild card. (Q) = Qualifier. (L) = Lucky loser.

The matches are the best of five sets

149

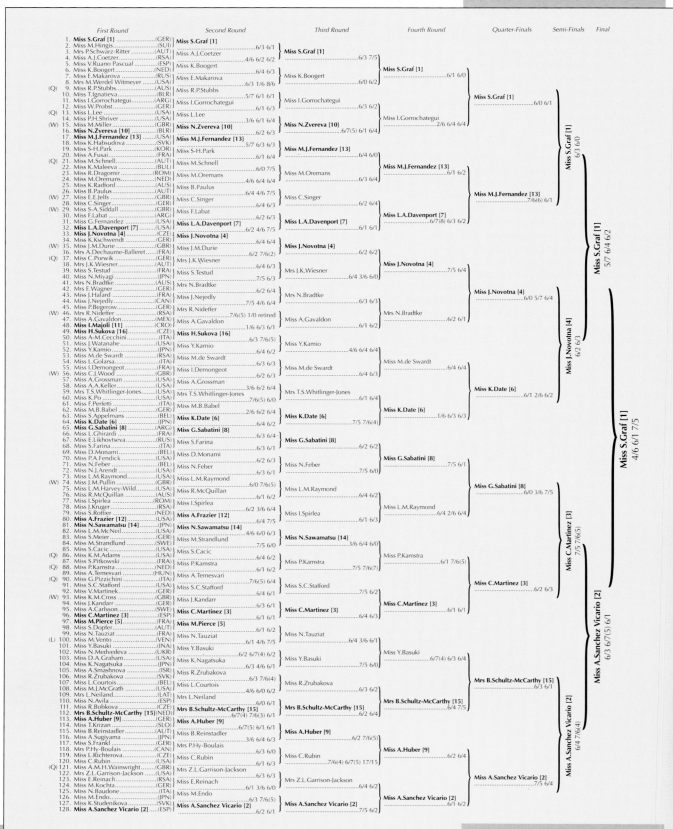

	First Round	Second Round	Third Round	Fourth Round	Quarter-Finals	Semi-Finals	Final

1. **Miss S.Graf [1]** .... (GER)
2. Miss M.Hingis .... (SUI)
3. Mrs P.Schwarz-Ritter .... (AUT)
4. Miss A.J.Coetzer .... (RSA)
5. Miss V.Ruano Pascual .... (ESP)
6. Miss K.Boogert .... (NED)
7. Miss E.Makarova .... (RUS)
8. Mrs M.Werdel Witmeyer .. (USA)
(Q) 9. Miss R.P.Stubbs .... (AUS)
10. Miss T.Ignatieva .... (BLR)
11. Miss I.Gorrochategui .... (ARG)
12. Miss W.Probst .... (GER)
(Q) 13. Miss L.Lee .... (USA)
14. Miss P.H.Shriver .... (USA)
(W) 15. Miss M.Miller .... (GBR)
16. **Miss N.Zvereva [10]** ..... (BLR)
17. **Miss M.J.Fernandez [13]** .... (USA)
18. Miss K.Habsudova .... (SVK)
19. Miss S-H.Park .... (KOR)
20. Miss A.Fusai .... (FRA)
(Q) 21. Miss M.Schnell .... (AUT)
22. Miss K.Maleeva .... (BUL)
23. Miss R.Dragomir .... (ROM)
24. Miss M.Oremans .... (NED)
25. Miss K.Radford .... (AUS)
26. Miss B.Paulus .... (AUT)
(W) 27. Miss E.E.Jelfs .... (GBR)
28. Miss C.Singer .... (GBR)
(W) 29. Miss S-A.Siddall .... (GBR)
30. Miss F.Labat .... (ARG)
31. Miss G.Fernandez .... (USA)
32. **Miss L.A.Davenport [7]** .. (USA)
33. **Miss J.Novotna [4]** .... (CZE)
34. Miss K.Kschwendt .... (GER)
(W) 35. Miss J.M.Durie .... (GBR)
36. Miss A.Dechaume-Balleret .. (FRA)
(Q) 37. Miss C.Porwik .... (GER)
38. Mrs J.K.Wiesner .... (AUT)
39. Miss S.Testud .... (FRA)
40. Miss N.Miyagi .... (JPN)
41. Mrs N.Bradtke .... (AUS)
42. Miss E.Wagner .... (GER)
43. Miss J.Halard .... (FRA)
44. Miss J.Nejedly .... (CAN)
45. Miss P.Begerow .... (GER)
(W) 46. Mrs R.Nideffer .... (RSA)
47. Miss A.Gavaldon .... (MEX)
48. **Miss I.Majoli [11]** .... (CRO)
49. **Miss H.Sukova [16]** ...... (CZE)
50. Miss A-M.Cecchini .... (ITA)
51. Miss J.Watanabe .... (USA)
52. Miss Y.Kamio .... (JPN)
53. Miss M.de Swardt .... (RSA)
54. Miss I.Golarsa .... (ITA)
55. Miss I.Demongeot .... (FRA)
(W) 56. Miss C.J.Wood .... (GBR)
57. Miss A.Grossman .... (USA)
58. Miss A.A.Keller .... (USA)
59. Mrs T.S.Whitlinger-Jones .. (USA)
60. Miss K.Po .... (USA)
61. Miss F.Perfetti .... (ITA)
62. Miss M.B.Babel .... (GER)
63. Miss S.Appelmans .... (BEL)
64. **Miss K.Date [6]** .... (JPN)
65. **Miss G.Sabatini [8]** ...... (ARG)
66. Miss L.Ghirardi .... (FRA)
67. Miss E.Likhovtseva .... (RUS)
68. Miss S.Farina .... (ITA)
69. Miss D.Monami .... (BEL)
70. Miss P.A.Fendick .... (USA)
71. Miss N.Feber .... (BEL)
72. Miss N.J.Arendt .... (USA)
73. Miss L.M.Raymond .... (USA)
(W) 74. Miss J.M.Pullin .... (GBR)
75. Miss L.M.Harvey-Wild .... (USA)
76. Miss R.McQuillan .... (AUS)
77. Miss I.Spirlea .... (ROM)
78. Miss J.Kruger .... (RSA)
79. Miss S.Rottier .... (NED)
80. **Miss A.Frazier [12]** ...... (USA)
81. **Miss N.Sawamatsu [14]** .. (JPN)
82. Miss L.M.McNeil .... (USA)
83. Miss S.Meier .... (GER)
84. Miss M.Strandlund .... (SWE)
85. Miss S.Cacic .... (USA)
(Q) 86. Miss K.M.Adams .... (USA)
87. Miss S.Pitkowski .... (FRA)
(Q) 88. Miss P.Kamstra .... (NED)
89. Miss A.Temesvari .... (HUN)
(Q) 90. Miss G.Pizzichini .... (ITA)
91. Miss S.C.Stafford .... (USA)
92. Miss V.Martinek .... (GER)
(W) 93. Miss K.M.Cross .... (GBR)
94. Miss J.Kandarr .... (GER)
95. Miss A.Carlsson .... (SWE)
96. **Miss C.Martinez [3]** ...... (ESP)
97. **Miss M.Pierce [5]** .... (FRA)
98. Miss S.Dopfer .... (AUT)
99. Miss N.Tauziat .... (FRA)
(L) 100. Miss M.Vento .... (VEN)
101. Miss Y.Basuki .... (INA)
102. Miss N.Medvedeva .... (UKR)
103. Miss D.A.Graham .... (USA)
104. Miss K.Nagatsuka .... (JPN)
105. Miss A.Smashnova .... (ISR)
106. Miss R.Zrubakova .... (SVK)
107. Miss L.Courtois .... (BEL)
108. Miss M.J.McGrath .... (USA)
109. Mrs L.Neiland .... (LAT)
110. Miss N.Avila .... (ESP)
111. Miss B.Bobkova .... (CZE)
112. **Mrs B.Schultz-McCarthy [15]** (NED)
113. **Miss A.Huber [9]** .... (GER)
114. Miss T.Krizan .... (SLO)
115. Miss B.Reinstadler .... (AUT)
116. Miss A.Sugiyama .... (JPN)
117. Miss S.Frankl .... (GER)
118. Miss P.Hy-Boulais .... (CAN)
119. Miss L.Richterova .... (CZE)
120. Miss C.Rubin .... (USA)
(Q) 121. Miss A.M.H.Wainwright .. (GBR)
122. Mrs Z.L.Garrison-Jackson .. (USA)
123. Miss E.Reinach .... (RSA)
124. Miss M.Kochta .... (GER)
125. Miss N.Baudone .... (ITA)
126. Miss M.Endo .... (JPN)
127. Miss K.Studenikova .... (SVK)
128. **Miss A.Sanchez Vicario [2]** .. (ESP)

Second Round

Miss S.Graf [1]
Miss A.J.Coetzer 6/3 6/1
Miss K.Boogert 4/6 6/2 6/2
Miss E.Makarova 6/4 6/3
Miss R.P.Stubbs 6/3 1/6 8/6
Miss I.Gorrochategui 5/7 6/1 6/1
Miss L.Lee
Miss N.Zvereva [10] 3/6 6/1 6/4
Miss M.J.Fernandez [13] 6/2 6/1
Miss S-H.Park 5/7 6/3 6/3
Miss M.Schnell 6/1 6/4
Miss M.Oremans 6/0 7/5
Miss B.Paulus 4/6 6/4 6/4
Miss C.Singer 6/4 4/6 7/5
Miss F.Labat 6/2 6/3
Miss L.A.Davenport [7] 6/2 4/6 7/5
Miss J.Novotna [4]
Miss J.M.Durie 6/4 6/4
Mrs J.K.Wiesner .... 6/2 7/6(2)
Miss S.Testud 6/4 6/3
Mrs N.Bradtke 7/5 6/3
Miss J.Nejedly 7/5 4/6 6/4
Mrs R.Nideffer .... 7/6(5) 1/0 retired
Miss A.Gavaldon 1/6 6/3 6/1
Miss H.Sukova [16]
Miss Y.Kamio .... 6/3 7/6(5)
Miss M.de Swardt 6/4 6/2
Miss I.Demongeot 6/3 6/4
Miss A.Grossman
Mrs T.S.Whitlinger-Jones 3/6 6/2 6/4
Miss M.B.Babel .... 7/6(5) 6/0
Miss K.Date [6] 2/6 6/2 6/4
Miss G.Sabatini [8] 6/4 6/2
Miss S.Farina 6/3 6/4
Miss D.Monami 6/3 6/1
Miss N.Feber 6/2 6/3
Miss L.M.Raymond
Miss R.McQuillan .... 6/0 7/6(5)
Miss I.Spirlea 6/1 6/2
Miss A.Frazier [12] 6/2 3/6 6/4
Miss N.Sawamatsu [14] 6/4 7/5
Miss S.Strandlund 4/6 6/0 6/4
Miss S.Cacic 7/5 6/4
Miss P.Kamstra 6/4 6/2
Miss A.Temesvari 6/1 6/2
Miss S.C.Stafford .... 7/6(5) 6/4
Miss J.Kandarr 6/4 6/4
Miss C.Martinez [3] 6/3 6/1
Miss M.Pierce [5] 6/1 6/1
Miss N.Tauziat 6/1 6/2
Miss Y.Basuki 6/1 4/6 7/5
Miss K.Nagatsuka .... 6/2 6/7(4) 6/2
Miss R.Zrubakova 6/3 4/6 6/1
Miss L.Courtois .... 6/3 7/6(4)
Mrs L.Neiland 4/6 6/0 6/2
Mrs B.Schultz-McCarthy [15] 6/0 6/2
Miss A.Huber [9] .... 6/7(4) 7/6(3) 6/1
Miss B.Reinstadler .... 6/7(5) 6/1 6/0
Mrs P.Hy-Boulais 3/6 6/4 6/3
Miss C.Rubin 6/3 6/0
Mrs Z.L.Garrison-Jackson 6/1 6/0
Miss E.Reinach 6/3 6/3
Miss M.Endo 6/1 3/6 6/0
Miss A.Sanchez Vicario [2] .... 6/3 7/6(5)

Third Round

Miss S.Graf [1] 6/3 7/5
Miss K.Boogert 6/0 6/2
Miss I.Gorrochategui 6/3 6/2
Miss N.Zvereva [10] .... 6/7(5) 6/1 6/4
Miss M.J.Fernandez [13] 6/4 6/0
Miss M.Oremans 6/3 6/4
Miss C.Singer 6/2 6/4
Miss L.A.Davenport [7] 6/1 6/1
Miss J.Novotna [4] 6/2 6/2
Mrs J.K.Wiesner 6/4 3/6 6/0
Mrs N.Bradtke 6/3 6/2
Miss A.Gavaldon 6/1 6/2
Miss Y.Kamio 4/6 6/4 6/4
Miss M.de Swardt 6/4 6/3
Mrs T.S.Whitlinger-Jones 6/1 6/4
Miss K.Date [6] .... 7/5 7/6(4)
Miss G.Sabatini [8] 6/2 6/2
Miss N.Feber 7/5 6/0
Miss L.M.Raymond 6/4 6/2
Miss I.Spirlea 6/1 6/2
Miss N.Sawamatsu [14] 3/6 6/4 6/0
Miss P.Kamstra .... 7/5 7/6(7)
Miss S.C.Stafford 7/5 6/2
Miss C.Martinez [3] 6/4 6/3
Miss N.Tauziat 6/4 3/6 6/1
Miss Y.Basuki 7/5 6/0
Miss R.Zrubakova 6/3 6/2
Mrs B.Schultz-McCarthy [15] 6/2 6/4
Miss A.Huber [9] .... 6/2 7/6(5)
Miss C.Rubin .... 7/6(4) 6/7(5) 17/15
Mrs Z.L.Garrison-Jackson 6/4 6/2
Miss A.Sanchez Vicario [2] 7/5 6/2

Fourth Round

Miss S.Graf [1] 6/1 6/0
Miss I.Gorrochategui 2/6 6/4 6/4
Miss M.J.Fernandez [13] 6/1 6/2
Miss L.A.Davenport [7] .... 6/7(8) 6/3 6/2
Miss J.Novotna [4] 7/5 6/4
Mrs N.Bradtke 6/2 6/1
Miss M.de Swardt 6/4 6/4
Miss K.Date [6] 1/6 6/3 6/3
Miss G.Sabatini [8] 7/5 6/1
Miss L.M.Raymond 6/4 2/6 6/4
Miss P.Kamstra .... 6/1 7/6(5)
Miss C.Martinez [3] 6/1 6/4
Miss Y.Basuki .... 6/7(4) 6/3 6/4
Mrs B.Schultz-McCarthy [15] .... 6/4 7/6(4)
Miss A.Huber [9] 6/2 6/4
Miss A.Sanchez Vicario [2] 6/1 6/2

Quarter-Finals

Miss S.Graf [1] 6/0 6/1
Miss M.J.Fernandez [13] .... 7/6(6) 6/1
Miss J.Novotna [4] 6/0 5/7 6/4
Miss K.Date [6] 6/1 2/6 6/2
Miss G.Sabatini [8] 6/0 3/6 7/5
Miss C.Martinez [3] 6/2 6/3
Miss A.Sanchez Vicario [2] 6/3 6/1

Semi-Finals

Miss S.Graf [1] 6/3 6/0
Miss J.Novotna [4] 6/2 6/3
Miss C.Martinez [3] .... 7/5 7/6(5)
Miss A.Sanchez Vicario [2] .... 6/4 7/6(4)

Semi-Finals (inner)

Miss S.Graf [1] 5/7 6/4 6/2
Miss A.Sanchez Vicario [2] .... 6/3 6/7(5) 6/1

Final

Miss S.Graf [1] 4/6 6/1 7/5

Holders: Miss G. Fernandez and Miss N. Zvereva

The winners become the holders, for one year only, of the CHALLENGE CUP presented by H.R.H. PRINCESS MARINA, DUCHESS OF KENT, the late President of The All England Lawn Tennis and Croquet Club. The winners also receive silver replicas of the Challenge Cup. A silver salver is presented to each of the runners-up and a bronze medal to each defeated semi-finalist.

First Round	Second Round	Third Round	Quarter-Finals	Semi-Finals	Final
1. **Miss G.Fernandez** (USA) & **Miss N.Zvereva** (BLR) .....[1]	Miss G.Fernandez (USA) & Miss N.Zvereva (BLR) [1]	Miss G.Fernandez (USA) & Miss N.Zvereva (BLR) [1]			
2. Miss M.Bernard (CAN) & Miss C.Delisle (CAN)	6/7(4) 6/0 6/4				
3. Miss K-A.Guse (AUS) & Miss V.Lake (GBR)	Miss K-A. Guse (AUS) & Miss V.Lake (GBR)	6/3 6/1			
(W) 4. Miss S-A.Siddall (GBR) & Miss A.M.H.Wainwright (GBR)	6/1 7/6(2)		Miss G.Fernandez (USA) & Miss N.Zvereva (BLR) [1]		
5. Miss M.Lindstrom (SWE) & Miss M.Strandlund (SWE)	Miss M.Lindstrom (SWE) & Miss M.Strandlund (SWE)	Miss K.Boogert (NED) & Mrs N.A.M.Muns-Jagerman (NED) [17]	6/2 6/2		
6. P.Langrova (CZE) & Miss H.Vildova (CZE)	5/7 6/1 6/1				
7. Miss C.Porwik (GER) & Miss C.Singer (GER)	Miss K.Boogert (NED) & Mrs N.A.M.Muns-Jagerman (NED) [17]	6/2 7/6(5)			
8. **Miss K.Boogert** (NED) & **Mrs N.A.M.Muns-Jagerman** (NED) [17]	7/5 6/4			Miss G.Fernandez (USA) & Miss N.Zvereva (BLR) [1]	
9. **Miss C.Martinez** (ESP) & **Miss P.Tarabini** (ARG) [11]	Miss C.Martinez (ESP) & Miss P.Tarabini (ARG) [11]	Miss C.Martinez (ESP) & Miss P.Tarabini (ARG) [11]		6/2 6/1	
(Q) 10. Miss K.Godridge (AUS) & Miss K.Sharpe (AUS)	4/6 3/6 10/8				
11. Miss K.Maleeva (BUL) & Miss N.Medvedeva (UKR)	Miss K.Maleeva (BUL) & Miss N.Medvedeva (UKR)	3/6 6/4 6/4			
12. Miss K.Kschwendt (GER) & Miss R.Simpson (CAN)	6/4 1/6 6/2		Miss C.Martinez (ESP) & Miss P.Tarabini (ARG) [11]		
13. Miss L.Horn (RSA) & Miss D.Monami (BEL)	Miss M.Hingis (SUI) & Miss R.Zrubakova (SVK)	Miss M.M.Bollegraf (NED) & Miss R.P.Stubbs (AUS) [7]	6/3 6/3		
14. Miss M.Hingis (SUI) & Miss R.Zrubakova (SVK)	6/1 6/7(2) 6/0				
15. Miss L.Courtois (BEL) & Miss N.Feber (BEL)	Miss M.M.Bollegraf (NED) & Miss R.P.Stubbs (AUS) [7]	3/6 6/4 6/2			
16. **Miss M.M.Bollegraf** (NED) & **Miss R.P.Stubbs** (AUS) .....[7]	6/1 6/3				
17. **Miss M.J.McGrath** (USA) & **Mrs L.Neiland** (LAT) .....[5]	Miss M.J.McGrath (USA) & Mrs L.Neiland (LAT) [5]	Miss M.J.McGrath (USA) & Mrs L.Neiland (LAT) [5]			Miss G.Fernandez (USA) & Miss N.Zvereva (BLR) [1]
18. Miss N.Dahlman (FIN) & Miss O.Lugina (UKR)	6/3 6/3				
19. Miss M.Paz (ARG) & Miss S.C.Stafford (USA)	Miss M.Paz (ARG) & Miss S.C.Stafford (USA)	6/1 6/0			
20. Miss E.Likhovtseva (RUS) & Mrs E.Wagner (GER)	6/3 7/5		Miss M.J.McGrath (USA) & Mrs L.Neiland (LAT) [5]		
21. Miss F.Golarsa (ITA) & Miss C.M.Vis (NED)	Miss M.B.Babel (GER) & Miss S.Farina (ITA)	Miss E.Reinach (RSA) & Miss I.Spirlea (ROM) [13]	6/2 6/4		
22. Miss B.Nagelsen (USA) & Miss R.M.White (USA)					
23. **Miss E.Reinach** (RSA) & **Miss I.Spirlea** (ROM) .....[13]	Miss E.Reinach (RSA) & Miss I.Spirlea (ROM) [13]	6/1 6/4			
24. **Miss E.Makarova** (RUS) & **Miss E.Maniokova** (RUS) .....[15]	6/2 6/7(4) 6/1			4/6 6/4 6/3	
25. Miss S.Appelmans (BEL) & Miss M.Oremans (NED)	Miss S.Appelmans (BEL) & Miss M.Oremans (NED)	Miss S.Appelmans (BEL) & Miss M.Oremans (NED)			
26. Miss J.M.Durie (GBR) & Miss C.J.Wood (GBR)	6/2 6/3				
27. Miss E.Melicharova (CZE) & Miss N.Van Lottum (FRA)	Miss J.M.Durie (GBR) & Miss C.J.Wood (GBR)	6/4 6/4			
28. Miss M.de Swardt (RSA) & Miss I.Majoli (CRO)	Miss M.de Swardt (RSA) & Miss I.Majoli (CRO)	Miss L.M.McNeil (USA) & Miss H.Sukova (CZE)	Miss L.M.McNeil (USA) & Miss H.Sukova (CZE)		
29. Miss D.A.Graham (USA) & Miss J.M.Hetherington (CAN)	4/6 6/2 6/4				
30. **Miss P.A.Fendick** (USA) & **Miss M.J.Fernandez** (USA) .....[6]	Miss L.M.McNeil (USA) & Miss H.Sukova (CZE)	6/7(5) 6/1 8/6	6/3 6/4		
31. **Miss L.M.McNeil** (USA) & **Miss H.Sukova** (CZE)	7/6(1) 3/6 7/5				
32. **Miss G.Sabatini** (ARG) & **Mrs B.Schultz-McCarthy** (NED) .....[9]	Miss G.Sabatini (ARG) & Mrs B.Schultz-McCarthy (NED) [9]	Miss G.Sabatini (ARG) & Mrs B.Schultz-McCarthy (NED) [9]			
33. Miss W.Probst (GER) & Miss D.Scott (USA)	6/2 6/4				
(W) 34. Miss M.Werdel Witmeyer (USA) & Mrs T.S.Whitlinger-Jones (USA)	Mrs M.Werdel Witmeyer (USA) & Mrs T.S.Whitlinger-Jones (USA)	3/6 6/4 6/4			
35. Miss J.M.Pullin (GBR) & Miss L.A.Woodroffe (GBR)	6/7(4) 6/1 6/3		Miss G.Sabatini (ARG) & Mrs B.Schultz-McCarthy (NED) [9]		
36. Miss A.Dechaume-Balleret (FRA) & Miss F.Labat (ARG)	Miss S.Amiach (FRA) & Miss S.Testud (FRA)	Miss J.Halard (FRA) & Miss N.Tauziat (FRA) [10]	6/1 7/6(2)		
37. Miss S.Amiach (FRA) & Miss S.Testud (FRA)	4/6 10/8				
38. Miss Y.Kamio (JPN) & Miss H.Nagano (JPN)	Miss J.Halard (FRA) & Miss N.Tauziat (FRA) [10]	6/0 6/2			
39. **Miss J.Halard** (FRA) & **Miss N.Tauziat** (FRA) .....[10]	6/2 6/4			Miss G.Sabatini (ARG) & Mrs B.Schultz-McCarthy (NED) [9]	
40. **Miss L.M.Harvey-Wild** (USA) & **Miss C.Rubin** (USA) .....[16]	Miss L.M.Harvey-Wild (USA) & Miss C.Rubin (USA) [16]	Miss A-M.Cecchini (ITA) & Miss I.Demongeot (FRA)	6/1 6/2		
41. Miss C.G.Barclay (AUS) & Mrs P.Hy-Boulais (CAN)					
42. Miss I.Driehuis (NED) & Miss L.Pleming (AUS)	Miss A-M.Cecchini (ITA) & Miss I.Demongeot (FRA)	1/6 6/3 6/4			
43. Miss A-M.Cecchini (ITA) & Miss I.Demongeot (FRA)	5/7 6/4 6/0		Miss A.Frazier (USA) & Miss K.Po (USA)		
44. Miss K.Nagatsuka (JPN) & Miss A.Sugiyama (JPN)	Miss A.Carlsson (SWE) & Miss A.Temesvari (HUN)	Miss A.Frazier (USA) & Miss K.Po (USA)	7/5 6/1		
45. Miss A.Carlsson (SWE) & Miss A.Temesvari (HUN)	7/6(5) 7/5				
46. Miss A.Frazier (USA) & Miss K.Po (USA)	Miss A.Frazier (USA) & Miss K.Po (USA)	6/2 6/4			
47. **Miss L.A.Davenport** (USA) & **Miss L.M.Raymond** (USA) .....[4]	6/7(4) 6/1				
48. **Miss N.J.Arendt** (USA) & **Miss P.H.Shriver** (USA) [8]	Miss N.J.Arendt (USA) & Miss P.H.Shriver (USA) [8]	Miss N.J.Arendt (USA) & Miss P.H.Shriver (USA) [8]			Miss J.Novotna (CZE) & Miss A.Sanchez Vicario (ESP) [2]
49. Miss L.Garrone (ITA) & Miss R.Grande (ITA)	6/4 6/2				
(L) 50. Miss J.Kruger (RSA) & Mrs P.Schwarz-Ritter (AUT)	Mrs N.Bradtke (AUS) & Miss K.Radford (AUS)	1/6 7/6(1) 11/9			
51. Mrs N.Bradtke (AUS) & Miss K.Radford (AUS)	6/4 6/2		Miss N.J.Arendt (USA) & Miss P.H.Shriver (USA) [8]		
52. Miss R.Bobkova (CZE) & Miss M.Koutstaal (NED)	Miss R.Bobkova (CZE) & Miss M.Koutstaal (NED)	Miss R.Bobkova (CZE) & Miss M.Koutstaal (NED)	6/3 7/5		
53. Miss R.Dragomir (ROM) & Miss A.Grossman (USA)	6/2 6/4				
(Q) 54. **Miss A.J.Coetzer** (RSA) & **Miss I.Gorrochategui** (ARG) .....[12]	Miss A.J.Coetzer (RSA) & Miss I.Gorrochategui (ARG) [12]	6/4 6/3			
55. **Miss K.M.Adams** (USA) & **Mrs Z.L.Garrison-Jackson** (USA) .....[14]	Miss K.M.Adams (USA) & Mrs Z.L.Garrison-Jackson (USA) [14]	Miss K.M.Adams (USA) & Mrs Z.L.Garrison-Jackson (USA) [14]		Miss J.Novotna (CZE) & Miss A.Sanchez Vicario (ESP) [2]	
56. Miss R.Hiraki (JPN) & Miss S-H.Park (KOR)	4/6 6/3				
57. Miss L.Poruri (USA) & Miss M.Tu (USA)	Miss A.Fusai (FRA) & Miss K.Habsudova (SVK)	6/0 6/0			
58. Miss A.Fusai (FRA) & Miss K.Habsudova (SVK)			Miss J.Novotna (CZE) & Miss A.Sanchez Vicario (ESP) [2]		
59. Miss E.S.H.Callens (BEL) & Miss R.McQuillan (AUS)	Miss E.S.H.Callens (BEL) & Miss R.McQuillan (AUS)	Miss J.Novotna (CZE) & Miss A.Sanchez Vicario (ESP) [2]	4/6 6/4 6/3		
(W) 60. Miss E.L.Bond (GBR) & Miss J.Moore (GBR)	6/1 6/1				
61. Miss Y.Basuki (INA) & Miss N.Miyagi (JPN)	Miss J.Novotna (CZE) & Miss A.Sanchez Vicario (ESP) [2]	7/6(5) 6/1			
62. **Miss J.Novotna** (CZE) & **Miss A.Sanchez Vicario** (ESP) .....[2]	6/2 6/3				

Results (right-hand bracket annotations):

Miss G.Fernandez (USA) & Miss N.Zvereva (BLR) [1] — 7/6(3) 6/7(7) 6/2

Miss M.J.McGrath (USA) & Mrs L.Neiland (LAT) [5] — 4/6 6/4 6/3

Miss G.Sabatini (ARG) & Mrs B.Schultz-McCarthy (NED) [9] — 6/1 7/6(2)

Miss J.Novotna (CZE) & Miss A.Sanchez Vicario (ESP) [2] — 7/6(5) 7/6 6/4

Miss G.Fernandez (USA) & Miss N.Zvereva (BLR) [1] — 7/6(5) 1/6 7/5 6/4

Miss J.Novotna (CZE) & Miss A.Sanchez Vicario (ESP) [2] — 5/7 7/5 6/4

Heavy type denotes seeded players. The encircled figure against names denotes the order in which they have been seeded.
(W) = Wild card. (Q) = Qualifier. (L) = Lucky loser.

The matches are the best of three sets

Holders: T.A. Woodbridge and Miss H. Sukova

The winners become the holders, for one year only, of the CHALLENGE CUP presented by the family of the late Mr S. H. Smith. The winners also receive silver replicas of the Challenge Cup. A silver salver is presented to each of the runners-up and a bronze medal to each defeated semi-finalist.

First Round	Second Round	Third Round	Quarter-Finals	Semi-Finals	Final
1. M.Woodforde (AUS) & Mrs L.Neiland (LAT) .....[1]	M.Woodforde (AUS) & Mrs L.Neiland (LAT) [1]	M.Woodforde (AUS) & Mrs L.Neiland (LAT) [1]	M.Woodforde (AUS) & Mrs L.Neiland (LAT) [1]	M.Woodforde (AUS) & Mrs L.Neiland (LAT) [1]	
2. K.Kinnear (USA) & Miss N.Miyagi (JPN)					
3. D.Randall (USA) & Miss W.Probst (GER)	D.Randall (USA) & Miss W.Probst (GER) 6/1 6/4				
4. H.J.Davids (NED) & Miss M.Oremans (NED)	6/4 7/6(4)	7/5 6/3			
5. P.Kilderry (AUS) & Miss R.M.White (USA)	B.Haygarth (RSA) & Miss C.Singer (GER)	B.Haygarth (RSA) & Miss C.Singer (GER)			
6. B.Haygarth (RSA) & Miss C.Singer (GER)	7/5 6/4	7/5 6/3			
7. J.Eagle (AUS) & Miss K.Radford (AUS)	J.Eagle (AUS) & Miss K.Radford (AUS)			6/4 7/5	
8. G.Van Emburgh (USA) & Miss N.J.Arendt (USA) .....[15]	4/6 7/6(5) 7/5		K.Jones (USA) & Miss K.M.Adams (USA)		
9. M.Jensen (USA) & Mrs B.Schultz-McCarthy (NED) .....[14]	M.Jensen (USA) & Mrs B.Schultz-McCarthy (NED) [14]	K.Jones (USA) & Miss K.M.Adams (USA)		6/2 6/1	
10. R.Bergh (SWE) & Mr R.P.Stubbs (AUS)	K.Jones (USA) & Miss K.M.Adams (USA) 6/3 6/3	default			
11. D.Johnson (USA) & Miss K.Kschwendt (GER)			A.Florent (AUS) & Miss C.G.Barclay (AUS)		
12. K.Jones (USA) & Miss K.M.Adams (USA)	A.Florent (AUS) & Miss C.G.Barclay (AUS)	A.Florent (AUS) & Miss C.G.Barclay (AUS)	6/3 7/5		
13. A.Florent (AUS) & Miss C.G.Barclay (AUS)	7/5 7/6(5)	3/6 7/5 11/9			
14. J.Ireland (AUS) & Miss K.Habsudova (SVK)	M.J.Bates (GBR) & Miss J.M.Durie (GBR)				
(W) 15. M.J.Bates (GBR) & Miss J.M.Durie (GBR)					
16. A.Olhovskiy (RUS) & Miss E.Maniokova (RUS) .....[8]					J.Stark (USA) & Miss M.Navratilova (USA) [3]
17. J.Stark (USA) & Miss M.Navratilova (USA) .....[3]	J.Stark (USA) & Miss M.Navratilova (USA) [3]	J.Stark (USA) & Miss M.Navratilova (USA) [3]	J.Stark (USA) & Miss M.Navratilova (USA) [3]	J.Stark (USA) & Miss M.Navratilova (USA) [3]	3/6 6/4 6/4
18. M.Lucena (USA) & Mrs T.S.Whitlinger-Jones (USA)	6/4 7/6(1)	6/4 7/5		7/6(4) 3/6 6/3	
19. S.Noteboom (NED) & Miss E.S.H.Callens (BEL)	S.Noteboom (NED) & Miss E.S.H.Callens (BEL)				
20. L.Pimek (BEL) & Miss N.Feber (BEL)	7/5 6/3		R.Leach (USA) & Miss N.Zvereva (BLR) [12]	6/3 6/3	
21. M.Barnard (RSA) & Miss N.A.M.Muns-Jagerman (USA)	J-L.De Jager (RSA) & Miss J.M.Hetherington (CAN)	R.Leach (USA) & Miss N.Zvereva (BLR) [12]			
22. J-L.De Jager (RSA) & Miss J.M.Hetherington (CAN)	6/2 7/5	6/2 7/6(5)			
23. M.Tebbutt (AUS) & Miss J.Halard (FRA)	R.Leach (USA) & Miss N.Zvereva (BLR) [12]				
24. R.Leach (USA) & Miss N.Zvereva (BLR) .....[12]					
25. S.Stolle (AUS) & Miss M.J.Fernandez (USA) .....[9]	S.Stolle (AUS) & Miss M.J.Fernandez (USA) [9]	S.Stolle (AUS) & Miss M.J.Fernandez (USA) [9]	S.Stolle (AUS) & Miss M.J.Fernandez (USA) [9]	S.Stolle (AUS) & Miss M.J.Fernandez (USA) [9]	
26. O.Kristiansson (SWE) & Miss M.Strandlund (SWE)	6/2 6/4	6/3 7/6(3)		6/4 7/6(4)	
27. K.Flach (USA) & Miss L.Poruri (USA)	D.Nargiso (ITA) & Miss A-M.Cecchini (ITA)				
28. D.Nargiso (ITA) & Miss A-M.Cecchini (ITA)			B.MacPhie (USA) & Miss L.M.Harvey-Wild (USA)		
(W) 29. P.T.Hand (GBR) & Miss V.Lake (GBR)	P.T.Hand (GBR) & Miss V.Lake (GBR)	B.MacPhie (USA) & Miss L.M.Harvey-Wild (USA)	6/4 7/5		
30. A.Kratzmann (AUS) & Miss D.Scott (USA)	7/6(6) 6/7(8) 6/3	6/3 6/3			
31. B.MacPhie (USA) & Miss L.M.Harvey-Wild (USA)	B.MacPhie (USA) & Miss L.M.Harvey-Wild (USA)				
32. L.J.Bale (RSA) & Miss M.J.McGrath (USA) .....[6]	6/2 4/6 6/3				
33. P.Galbraith (USA) & Miss E.Reinach (RSA) .....[7]	D.T.Visser (RSA) & Miss I.Spirlea (ROM)	T.Nijssen (NED) & Miss C.Porwik (GER)	T.Nijssen (NED) & Miss C.Porwik (GER)	T.Nijssen (NED) & Miss C.Porwik (GER)	
34. D.T.Visser (RSA) & Miss I.Spirlea (ROM)	6/3 6/4	3/6 7/6(2) 8/6	7/6(9) 6/2		
35. T.Nijssen (NED) & Miss C.Porwik (GER)	T.Nijssen (NED) & Miss C.Porwik (GER)				
36. P.Norval (RSA) & Miss S.Amiach (FRA)	6/4 6/4				
37. E.Ferreira (RSA) & Mrs P.Hy-Boulais (CAN)	P.Albano (ARG) & Miss M.Paz (ARG)	P.Albano (ARG) & Miss M.Paz (ARG)			
38. P.Albano (ARG) & Miss M.Paz (ARG)	6/3 6/4	6/4 6/4			
39. W.Arthurs (AUS) & Miss K-A.Guse (AUS)	W.Arthurs (AUS) & Miss K-A.Guse (AUS)				
40. J.B.Fitzgerald (AUS) & Miss M.M.Bollegraf (NED) .....[11]	6/4 4/6 6/2		D.Norman (BEL) & Miss S.Appelmans (BEL)		
41. D.Macpherson (AUS) & Miss R.McQuillan (AUS) .....[16]	D.Norman (BEL) & Miss S.Appelmans (BEL)	D.Norman (BEL) & Miss S.Appelmans (BEL)	5/7 6/3 6/4		
42. D.Norman (BEL) & Miss S.Appelmans (BEL)	7/6(5) 6/4	5/7 6/3 6/4			
43. L.B.Jensen (USA) & Miss R.Jensen (USA)	L.B.Jensen (USA) & Miss R.Jensen (USA)				C.Suk (CZE) & Miss G.Fernandez (USA) [4]
44. J.Waite (USA) & Miss S.C.Stafford (USA)	6/3 6/4				
(W) 45. D.E.Sapsford (GBR) & Miss S-A.Siddall (GBR)	L.Lavalle (MEX) & Miss D.Monami (BEL)	C.Suk (CZE) & Miss G.Fernandez (USA) [4]	C.Suk (CZE) & Miss G.Fernandez (USA) [4]	C.Suk (CZE) & Miss G.Fernandez (USA) [4]	
46. L.Lavalle (MEX) & Miss D.Monami (BEL)	2/6 6/1 1/1 retired	6/1 6/4		6/4 6/3	
47. K.Thorne (USA) & Miss A.Fusai (FRA)	C.Suk (CZE) & Miss G.Fernandez (USA) [4]				
48. C.Suk (CZE) & Miss G.Fernandez (USA) .....[4]	6/4 6/3				
49. D.Adams (RSA) & Miss L.M.Raymond (USA) .....[5]	T.J.Middleton (USA) & Miss L.M.McNeil (USA)	T.J.Middleton (USA) & Miss L.M.McNeil (USA)	M.R.J.Petchey (GBR) & Miss C.J.Wood (GBR)		
50. T.J.Middleton (USA) & Miss L.M.McNeil (USA)	6/4 6/3	6/3 7/6(4)	6/4 7/5		
51. T.A.Woodbridge (AUS) & Miss H.Sukova (CZE)	T.A.Woodbridge (AUS) & Miss H.Sukova (CZE)				
52. M.Bauer (USA) & Miss P.A.Fendick (USA)	6/3 6/7(6) 6/1				
(W) 53. C.Wilkinson (GBR) & Miss A.M.H.Wainwright (GBR)	M.R.J.Petchey (GBR) & Miss C.J.Wood (GBR)	M.R.J.Petchey (GBR) & Miss C.J.Wood (GBR)			
(W) 54. M.R.J.Petchey (GBR) & Miss C.M.Vis (NED)		4/6 6/2 6/4			
55. T.Kempers (NED) & Miss C.M.Vis (NED)	M.Oosting (NED) & Miss K.Boogert (NED) [13]				
56. M.Oosting (NED) & Miss K.Boogert (NED) .....[13]					
57. B.Steven (NZL) & Mrs N.Bradtke (AUS) .....[10]	B.Steven (NZL) & Mrs N.Bradtke (AUS) [10]	B.Steven (NZL) & Mrs N.Bradtke (AUS) [10]	G.Connell (CAN) & Miss L.A.Davenport (USA) [2]	G.Connell (CAN) & Miss L.A.Davenport (USA) [2]	
58. L-A.Wahlgren (SWE) & Miss M.Lindstrom (SWE)	7/5 6/3	7/6(2) 7/5	5/7 6/4 6/3		
59. M.Ondruska (RSA) & Miss L.Pleming (AUS)	J.Frana (ARG) & Miss P.Tarabini (ARG)				
60. J.Frana (ARG) & Miss P.Tarabini (ARG)	1/6 7/5 6/2				
61. C.Brandi (ITA) & Miss L.Golarsa (ITA)	S.E.Davis (USA) & Miss D.A.Graham (USA)	G.Connell (CAN) & Miss L.A.Davenport (USA) [2]			
62. S.E.Davis (USA) & Miss D.A.Graham (USA)	6/4 6/3	4/6 6/3 7/5			
63. N.Broad (GBR) & Miss R.Simpson (CAN)	G.Connell (CAN) & Miss L.A.Davenport (USA) [2]				
64. G.Connell (CAN) & Miss L.A.Davenport (USA) .....[2]	6/2 6/4				

Heavy type denotes seeded players. The encircled figure against names denotes the order in which they have been seeded.
(W) = Wild card. (Q) = Qualifier. (L) = Lucky loser.
The matches are the best of three sets

Holders: J.D. Newcombe and A.D. Roche

The winners become the holders, for one year only, of a Cup presented by The All England Lawn Tennis and Croquet Club. The winners also receive miniature silver salvers. A silver medal is presented to each of the runners-up.

First Round	Second Round	Semi-Finals	Final
1. J.D.Newcombe (AUS) & A.D.Roche (AUS) .....[1]	J.D.Newcombe (AUS) & A.D.Roche (AUS) [1]	J.D.Newcombe (AUS) & A.D.Roche (AUS) [1]	J.D.Newcombe (AUS) & A.D.Roche (AUS) [1]
2. bye			
3. J.Kodes (CZE) & A.Metreveli (RUS)	J.Kodes (CZE) & A.Metreveli (RUS)		
4. G.Battrick (GBR) & M.Cox (GBR)	6/3 6/2	6/7(10) 6/1 6/3	
5. I.Nastase (ROM) & T.S.Okker (NED) .....[4]	I.Nastase (ROM) & T.S.Okker (NED) [4]	R.A.J.Hewitt (RSA) & F.D.McMillan (RSA)	
6. bye		6/4 1/6 6/3	7/6(2) 6/3
7. R.A.J.Hewitt (RSA) & F.D.McMillan (RSA)	R.A.J.Hewitt (RSA) & F.D.McMillan (RSA)		
8. P.C.Dent (AUS) & A.J.Stone (AUS)	3/6 7/6(5) 7/5		
9. J.R.Cooper (AUS) & N.A.Fraser (AUS)	N.Pilic (CRO) & S.R.Smith (USA)		
10. N.Pilic (CRO) & S.R.Smith (USA)	6/1 6/2	O.K.Davidson (AUS) & E.C.Drysdale (RSA) [3]	
11. bye		6/2 7/6(8)	
12. O.K.Davidson (AUS) & E.C.Drysdale (RSA) .....[3]	O.K.Davidson (AUS) & E.C.Drysdale (RSA) [3]		O.K.Davidson (AUS) & E.C.Drysdale (RSA) [3]
13. M.Santana (ESP) & R.Taylor (GBR)	M.C.Riessen (USA) & S.E.Stewart (USA)		6/3 7/6(0)
14. M.C.Riessen (USA) & S.E.Stewart (USA)	6/4 6/3	M.C.Riessen (USA) & S.E.Stewart (USA)	
15. bye		6/3 6/1	
16. K.R.Rosewall (AUS) & F.S.Stolle (AUS) .....[2]	K.R.Rosewall (AUS) & F.S.Stolle (AUS) [2]		

Heavy type denotes seeded players. The figure in brackets against names denotes the order in which they have been seeded. The matches will be the best of three sets. The tie-break will operate at six games all in the first two sets.

Heavy type denotes seeded players. The encircled figure against names denotes the order in which they have been seeded.
The matches are the best of three sets

THE 35 AND OVER GENTLEMEN'S INVITATION DOUBLES

The winners become the holders, for one year only, of a cup presented by The All England Lawn Tennis and Croquet Club. The winners also receive miniature silver salvers. A silver medal is presented to each of the runners-up.

Holders: H.P. Guenthardt and B. Taroczy

GROUP A

Pair	v	Match 1	Match 2	Match 3	Wins	Losses
P. B. McNamara (AUS) & **L. Shiras** (USA)	v	T. R. Gullikson (USA) & R. L. Stockton (USA) 2/6 7/5 9/7	R. J. Frawley (AUS) & C. J. Lewis (NZL) 4/6 6/7(5)	C. Dowdeswell (GBR) & C. J. Mottram (GBR) 7/5 6/7(13) 16/14	2	1
R. J. Frawley (AUS) & C. J. Lewis (NZL)	v	C. Dowdeswell (GBR) & C. J. Mottram (GBR) 6/7(3) 3/6	**P. B. McNamara** (AUS) **& L. Shiras** (USA) 6/4 7/6(5)	T. R. Gullikson (USA) & R. L. Stockton (USA) 2/6 3/6	1	2
C. Dowdeswell (GBR) & C. J. Mottram (GBR)	v	R. J. Frawley (AUS) & C. J. Lewis (NZL) 7/6(3) 6/3	T. R. Gullikson (USA) & R. L. Stockton (USA) 3/6 6/3 3/6	**P. B. McNamara** (AUS) **& L. Shiras** (USA) 5/7 7/6(13) 14/16	1	2
T. R. Gullikson (USA) & R. L. Stockton (USA)	v	**P. B. McNamara** (AUS) **& L. Shiras** (USA) 6/2 5/7 7/9	C. Dowdeswell (GBR) & C. J. Mottram (GBR) 6/3 3/6 6/3	R. J. Frawley (AUS) & C. J. Lewis (NZL) 6/2 6/3	2	1

GROUP B

Pair	v	Match 1	Match 2	Match 3	Wins	Losses
H. Guenthardt (SUI) & **G. Vilas** (ARG)	v	J. G. Alexander (AUS) & T. Wilkison (USA) 1/6 4/6	B. E. Gottfried (USA) & R. Ramirez (MEX) 2/6 5/7	A. A. Mayer (USA) & G. Mayer (USA) 4/6 2/6	0	3
J. G. Alexander (AUS) & T. Wilkison (USA)	v	**H. Guenthardt** (SUI) & **G. Vilas** (ARG) 6/1 6/4	A. A. Mayer (USA) & G. Mayer (USA) 6/4 6/7(8) 3/6	B. E. Gottfried (USA) & R. Ramirez (MEX) 4/6 6/7(7)	1	2
B. E. Gottfried (USA) & R. Ramirez (MEX)	v	A. A. Mayer (USA) & G. Mayer (USA) 6/4 6/4	**H. Guenthardt** (SUI) & **G. Vilas** (ARG) 6/2 7/5	J. G. Alexander (AUS) & T. Wilkison (USA) 6/4 7/6(7)	3	0
A. A. Mayer (USA) & G. Mayer (USA)	v	B. E. Gottfried (USA) & R. Ramirez (MEX) 4/6 4/6	J. G. Alexander (AUS) & T. Wilkison (USA) 4/6 7/6(8) 6/3	**H. Guenthardt** (SUI) & **G. Vilas** (ARG) 6/4 6/2	2	1

GROUP C

Pair	v	Match 1	Match 2	Match 3	Wins	Losses
A. M. Jarrett (GBR) & **J. R. Smith** (GBR)	v	M. Bahrami (IRN) & J. Higueras (ESP) 5/7 3/6	P. Dupre (USA) & H. Solomon (USA) 4/6 6/4 6/4	M. R. Edmondson (AUS) & K. Warwick (AUS) 3/6 5/7	1	2
P. Dupre (USA) & H. Solomon (USA)	v	M. R. Edmondson (AUS) & K. Warwick (AUS) 1/6 4/6	**A. M. Jarrett** (GBR) & **J. R. Smith** (GBR) 6/4 4/6 4/6	M. Bahrami (IRN) & J. Higueras (ESP) 3/6 6/7(5)	0	3
M. Bahrami (IRN) & J. Higueras (ESP)	v	**A. M. Jarrett** (GBR) & **J. R. Smith** (GBR) 7/5 6/3	M. R. Edmondson (AUS) & K. Warwick (AUS) 3/6 6/2 6/3	P. Dupre (USA) & H. Solomon (USA) 6/3 7/6(5)	3	0
M. R. Edmondson (AUS) & K. Warwick (AUS)	v	P. Dupre (USA) & H. Solomon (USA) 6/1 6/4	M. Bahrami (IRN) & J. Higueras (ESP) 6/3 2/6 3/6	**A. M. Jarrett** (GBR) & **J. R. Smith** (GBR) 6/3 7/5	2	1

GROUP D

Pair	v	Match 1	Match 2	Match 3	Wins	Losses
P. Fleming (USA) & **H. Pfister** (USA)	v	A. Amritraj (IND) & V. Amritraj (IND) 4/6 4/6	P. Slozil (CZE) & T. Smid (CZE) 3/6 6/3 6/4	R. L. Case (AUS) & G. Masters (AUS) 7/6(7) 6/2	2	1
A. Amritraj (IND) & V. Amritraj (IND)	v	**P. Fleming** (USA) & **H. Pfister** (USA) 6/4 6/4	R. L. Case (AUS) & G. Masters (AUS) 6/4 6/2	P. Slozil (CZE) & T. Smid (CZE) 1/6 7/6(6) 7/5	3	0
R. L. Case (AUS) & G. Masters (AUS)	v	P. Slozil (CZE) & T. Smid (CZE) 1/6 1/6	A. Amritraj (IND) & V. Amritraj (IND) 4/6 2/6	**P. Fleming** (USA) & **H. Pfister** (USA) 6/7(7) 2/6	0	3
P. Slozil (CZE) & T. Smid (CZE)	v	R. L. Case (AUS) & G. Masters (AUS) 6/1 6/1	**P. Fleming** (USA) & **H. Pfister** (USA) 6/3 3/6 4/6	A. Amritraj (IND) & V. Amritraj (IND) 6/1 6/7(6) 5/7	1	2

SEMI-FINAL

P. B. McNamara (AUS) & L. Shiras (USA) — B. E. Gottfried (USA) & R. Ramirez (MEX) — 7/6(2) 6/3

M. Bahrami (IRN) & J. Higueras (ESP) — A. Amritraj (IND) & V. Amritraj (IND) — 4/6 6/3 6/4

FINAL

P. B. McNamara (AUS) & L. Shiras (USA) — M. Bahrami (IRN) & J. Higueras (ESP) — 7/6(10) 7/5

This event will be played on a 'round robin' basis. 16 invited pairs have been divided into 4 groups and each pair in each group will play one another. The pairs winning most matches will be the winners of their respective groups and will play semi-final and final rounds as indicated above.
If matches should be equal in any group, the head to head result between the two pairs with the same number of wins, will determine the winning pair of the group.
Heavy type denotes seeded players. The figure in brackets against names denotes the order in which they have been seeded. The matches will be the best of three sets. The tie-break will operate at six games all in the first two sets.

This event is played on a 'round robin' basis. Sixteen invited pairs are divided into four groups and each pair in each group plays the others. The pairs winning most matches are the winners of their respective groups and play semi-final and final rounds as indicated above.
If matches should be equal in any group, the head-to-head result between the two pairs with the same number of wins determines the winning pair of the group.

Heavy type denotes seeded players. The encircled figure against names denotes the order in which they have been seeded.

The matches are the best of three sets

The winners become the holders, for one year only, of a cup presented by The All England Lawn Tennis and Croquet Club. The winners also receive miniature cups. A silver medal is presented to each of the runners-up.

Holders: Miss W.M. Turnbull and Miss S.V. Wade

Play-Back Final	Play-Back Semi-Finals	First Round	Semi-Finals	Final
	Miss H.Gourlay (AUS) & Mrs G.E.Reid (AUS) 1/6 1/6	**Miss W.M.Turnbull** (AUS) & **Miss S.V.Wade** (GBR) [1] v Miss H.Gourlay (AUS) & Mrs G.E.Reid (AUS)	**Miss W.M.Turnbull** (AUS) & **Miss S.V.Wade** (GBR) [1] 6/1 6/1	**Miss W.M.Turnbull** (AUS) & **Miss S.V.Wade** (GBR) [1] 6/1 6/2
Mrs O.Morozova (RUS) & Miss B.F.Stove (NED) [4] 6/4 6/2	**Mrs O.Morozova** (RUS) & **Miss B.F.Stove** (NED) [4] 0/6 0/6	**Mrs O.Morozova** (RUS) & **Miss B.F.Stove** (NED) [4] v Mrs A.K.Hayashi (USA) & Miss Y.Vermaak (RSA)	Mrs A.K.Hayashi (USA) & Miss Y.Vermaak (RSA) 6/0 6/0	
Miss R.Casals (USA) & Mrs R.Cawley (AUS) 6/4 6/4	Miss R.Casals (USA) & Mrs R.Cawley (AUS) 0/6 4/6	Miss R.Casals (USA) & Mrs R.Cawley (AUS) v **Miss L.J.Charles** (GBR) & **Miss A.Hobbs** (GBR) [3]	**Miss L.J.Charles** (GBR) & **Miss A.Hobbs** (GBR) [3] 6/0 6/4	**Miss B.Nagelsen** (USA) & **Miss J.C.Russell** (USA) [2] 6/2 3/6 6/2
Miss R.Casals (USA) & Mrs R.Cawley (AUS) 6/4 6/7(5) 9/7	Miss F.Durr (FRA) & Miss M.Jausovec (SLO) 3/6 1/6	Miss F.Durr (FRA) & Miss M.Jausovec (SLO) v **Miss B.Nagelsen** (USA) & **Miss J.C.Russell** (USA) [2]	**Miss B.Nagelsen** (USA) & **Miss J.C.Russell** (USA) [2] 6/3 6/1	**Miss W.M.Turnbull** (AUS) & **Miss S.V.Wade** (GBR) [1] 6/3 7/6(5)

Heavy type denotes seeded players. The encircled figure against names denotes the order in which they have been seeded. There are play-back matches for first-round losers.
The matches are the best of three sets

ALPHABETICAL LIST – 35 & OVER EVENTS

GENTLEMEN

Alexander, J.G. (Australia)	Fleming, P. (USA)	Masters, G. (Australia)	Slozil, P. (Czech Republic)
Amritraj, A. (India)	Frawley, R.J. (Australia)	Mayer, A.A. (USA)	Smid, T. (Czech Republic)
Amritraj, V. (India)	Gottfried, B.E. (USA)	Mayer, G. (USA)	Smith, J.R. (Great Britain)
Bahrami, M. (Iran)	Guenthardt, H. (Switzerland)	McNamara, P.B. (Australia)	Solomon, H. (USA)
Case, R.L. (Australia)	Gullikson, T.R. (USA)	Mottram, C.J. (Great Britain)	Stockton, R.L. (USA)
Dowdeswell, C. (Great Britain)	Higueras, J. (Spain)	Pfister, H. (USA)	Vilas, G. (Argentina)
Dupre, P. (USA)	Jarrett, A.M. (Great Britain)	Ramirez, R. (Mexico)	Warwick, K. (Australia)
Edmondson, M.R. (Australia)	Lewis, C.J. (New Zealand)	Shiras, L. (USA)	Wilkison, T. (USA)

LADIES

Casals, Miss R. (USA)	Gourlay, Miss H. (Australia)	Morozova, Mrs O. (Russia)	Stove, Miss B.F. (Netherlands)
Cawley, Mrs R. (Australia)	Hayashi, Mrs A.K. (USA)	Nagelsen, Miss B. (USA)	Turnbull, Miss W.M. (Australia)
Charles, Miss L.J. (Great Britain)	Hobbs, Miss A. (Great Britain)	Reid, Mrs G.E. (Australia)	Vermaak, Miss Y. (South Africa)
Durr, Miss F. (France)	Jausovec, Miss M. (Slovenia)	Russell, Miss J.C. (USA)	Wade, Miss S.V. (Great Britain)

ALPHABETICAL LIST – 45 & OVER EVENT

GENTLEMEN

Battrick, G. (Great Britain)	Fraser, N.A. (Australia)	Newcombe, J.D. (Australia)	Santana, M. (Spain)
Cooper, J.R. (Australia)	Hewitt, R.A.J. (South Africa)	Okker, T.S. (Netherlands)	Smith, S.R. (USA)
Cox, M. (Great Britain)	Kodes, J. (Czech Republic)	Pilic, N. (Croatia)	Stewart, S.E. (USA)
Davidson, O.K. (Australia)	McMillan, F.D. (South Africa)	Riessen, M.C. (USA)	Stolle, F.S. (Australia)
Dent, P.C. (Australia)	Metreveli, A. (Russia)	Roche, A.D. (Australia)	Stone, A.J. (Australia)
Drysdale, E.C. (South Africa)	Nastase, I. (Romania)	Rosewall, K.R. (Australia)	Taylor, R. (Great Britain)

Holder: S. Humphries

For both the Boys' Singles *and the* Boys' Doubles Championships, the winners become the holders, for one year only, of a cup presented by The All England Lawn Tennis and Croquet Club. The winners and runners-up each receive a personal prize.

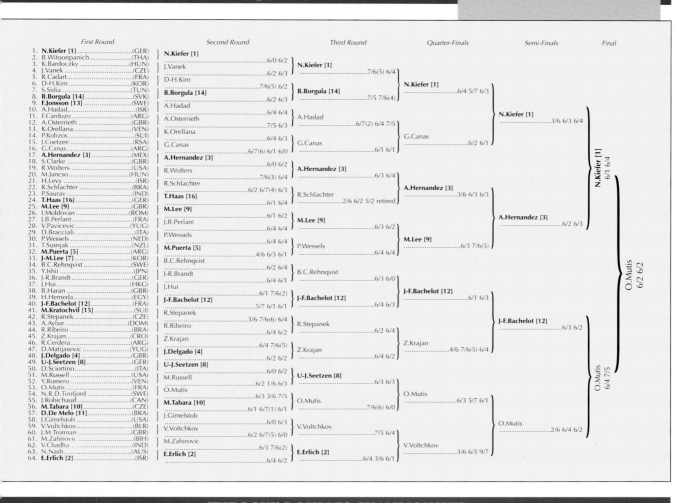

First Round	Second Round	Third Round	Quarter-Finals	Semi-Finals	Final
1. **N.Kiefer [1]** (GER)	N.Kiefer [1]				
2. B.Witoonpanich (THA)	...........6/0 6/2	N.Kiefer [1]			
3. K.Bardoczky (HUN)	J.Vanek	...........7/6(5) 6/4	N.Kiefer [1]		
4. J.Vanek (CZE)	...........6/2 6/3				
5. R.Cadart (FRA)	D-H.Kim				
6. D-H.Kim (KOR)	...........7/6(5) 6/2	B.Borgula [14]			
7. S.Sidia (TUN)	B.Borgula [14]	...........7/5 7/6(4)		N.Kiefer [1]	
8. **B.Borgula [14]** (SVK)	...........6/2 6/3			...........3/6 6/3 6/4	
9. **F.Jonsson [13]** (SWE)	A.Hadad				
10. A.Hadad (ISR)	...........6/4 6/4	A.Hadad			
11. F.Cardozo (ARG)	A.Osterrieth	...........6/7(2) 6/4 7/5	G.Canas		
12. A.Osterrieth (GBR)	...........7/5 6/3		...........6/2 6/1		
13. K.Orellana (VEN)	K.Orellana				
14. P.Kobzos (SUI)	...........6/4 6/4	G.Canas			
15. J.Coetzee (RSA)	G.Canas	...........6/1 6/1			
16. G.Canas (ARG)	...........6/7(6) 6/1 6/0				
17. **A.Hernandez [3]** (MEX)	A.Hernandez [3]				
18. S.Clarke (GBR)	...........6/0 6/2	A.Hernandez [3]			
19. R.Wolters (USA)	R.Wolters	...........6/3 6/4			
20. M.Jancso (HUN)	...........7/6(3) 6/4		A.Hernandez [3]		
21. H.Levy (ISR)	R.Schlachter		...........3/6 6/3 6/3		
22. R.Schlachter (BRA)	...........6/2 6/7(4) 6/3	T.Haas [16]			
23. P.Saurav (IND)	T.Haas [16]	...........2/6 6/2 5/2 retired			
24. **T.Haas [16]** (GER)	...........6/1 6/4			A.Hernandez [3]	
25. **M.Lee [9]** (GBR)	M.Lee [9]			...........6/2 6/3	
26. I.Moldovan (ROM)	...........6/1 6/2	M.Lee [9]			
27. J.B.Perlant (FRA)	J.B.Perlant	...........6/3 6/2			
28. V.Pavicevic (YUG)	...........6/4 6/4		M.Lee [9]		
29. D.Bracciali (ITA)	P.Wessels		...........6/3 7/6(5)		
30. P.Wessels (NED)	...........6/4 6/4	P.Wessels			
31. T.Susnjak (NZL)	M.Puerta [5]	...........6/4 6/4			
32. **M.Puerta [5]** (ARG)	...........4/6 6/3 6/1				
33. **J-M.Lee [7]** (KOR)	B.C.Rehnqvist				
34. B.C.Rehnqvist (SWE)	...........6/2 6/4	B.C.Rehnqvist			
35. Y.Ishii (JPN)	J-R.Brandt	...........6/3 6/0			
36. J-R.Brandt (GER)	...........6/4 6/1		J-F.Bachelot [12]		
37. J.Hui (HKG)	J.Hui		...........6/1 6/3		
38. B.Haran (GBR)	...........6/1 7/6(2)	J-F.Bachelot [12]			
39. H.Hemeda (EGY)	J-F.Bachelot [12]	...........6/4 6/3			
40. **J-F.Bachelot [12]** (FRA)	...........5/7 6/1 6/1			J-F.Bachelot [12]	
41. **M.Kratochvil [15]** (SUI)	R.Stepanek			...........6/3 6/2	
42. R.Stepanek (CZE)	...........3/6 7/6(6) 6/4	R.Stepanek			
43. A.Aybar (DOM)	R.Ribeiro	...........6/2 6/4			
44. R.Ribeiro (BRA)	...........6/4 6/4		Z.Krajan		
45. Z.Krajan (CRO)	Z.Krajan		...........4/6 7/6(5) 6/4		
46. R.Cerdera (ARG)	...........6/4 7/6(5)	Z.Krajan			
47. D.Matijasevic (YUG)	J.Delgado [4]	...........6/4 6/2			
48. **J.Delgado [4]** (GBR)	...........6/2 6/2				
49. **U-J.Seetzen [8]** (GER)	U-J.Seetzen [8]				
50. D.Sciortino (ITA)	...........6/0 6/2	U-J.Seetzen [8]			
51. M.Russell (USA)	M.Russell	...........6/3 6/3			
52. Y.Romero (VEN)	...........6/2 1/6 6/3		O.Mutis		
53. O.Mutis (FRA)	O.Mutis		...........6/3 5/7 6/1		
54. N.R.D.Timfjord (SWE)	...........6/3 3/6 7/5	O.Mutis			
55. J.Robichaud (CAN)	M.Tabara [10]	...........7/6(6) 6/0			
56. **M.Tabara [10]** (CZE)	...........6/1 6/7(1) 6/1			O.Mutis	
57. **D.De Melo [11]** (BRA)	J.Gimelstob			...........2/6 6/4 6/2	
58. J.Gimelstob (USA)	...........6/0 6/3	V.Voltchkov			
59. V.Voltchkov (BLR)	V.Voltchkov	...........7/5			
60. J.M.Trotman (GBR)	...........6/2 6/7(5) 6/0		V.Voltchkov		
61. M.Zahirovic (BIH)	M.Zahirovic		...........3/6 6/3 9/7		
62. V.Chadha (IND)	...........6/3 7/6(2)	E.Erlich [2]			
63. N.Nash (AUS)	E.Erlich [2]	...........6/4 3/6 6/1			
64. **E.Erlich [2]** (ISR)	...........6/4 6/2				

Final winner: N.Kiefer [1] — 6/1 6/4
O.Mutis — 6/2 6/2

Holders: B. Ellwood and M. Philippoussis

First Round	Second Round	Quarter-Finals	Semi-Finals	Final
1. **E.Erlich** (ISR) **& K.Orellana** (VEN) [1]	B.Borgula (SVK) & M.Zahirovic (BIH)			
2. B.Borgula (SVK) & M.Zahirovic (BIH)	...........7/5 6/7(1) 6/4	M.Lee (GBR) & J.M.Trotman (GBR)		
3. A.Aybar (DOM) & Y.Romero (VEN)	M.Lee (GBR) & J.M.Trotman (GBR)			
4. M.Lee (GBR) & J.M.Trotman (GBR)	...........6/4 6/2	...........6/3 6/7(6) 6/2	M.Lee (GBR) & J.M.Trotman (GBR)	
5. A.Hadad (ISR) & H.Levy (ISR)	A.Hadad (ISR) & H.Levy (ISR)			
6. L.Bourgeois (AUS) & M.Nielsen (NZL)	...........6/4 7/5	A.Hadad (ISR) & H.Levy (ISR)	...........6/2 6/2	
7. F.Cardozo (ARG) & R.Cerdera (ARG)	J-R.Brandt (GER) & P.Wessels (NED) [7]			
8. **J-R.Brandt** (GER) **& P.Wessels** (NED) [7]	...........6/3 6/1	...........6/4 3/6 8/6		
9. **G.Canas** (ARG) **& M.Garcia** (ARG) [4]	G.Canas (ARG) & M.Garcia (ARG) [4]			
10. S.Clarke (GBR) & M.Woolley (GBR)	...........6/4 6/4	G.Canas (ARG) & M.Garcia (ARG) [4]		
11. J.Robichaud (CAN) & T.Susnjak (NZL)	J.Robichaud (CAN) & T.Susnjak (NZL)			
12. Z.Krajan (CRO) & I.Moldovan (ROM)	...........6/4 0/6 6/3	...........6/4 3/6 6/1	J.Gimelstob (USA) & R.Wolters (USA) [8]	
13. B.Haran (GBR) & S.T.Pender (GBR)	B.Haran (GBR) & S.T.Pender (GBR)			
14. V.Chadha (IND) & M.Jancso (HUN)	...........7/5 6/3	J.Gimelstob (USA) & R.Wolters (USA) [8]	...........6/3 6/2	
15. J.Coetzee (RSA) & D.Roberts (RSA)	J.Gimelstob (USA) & R.Wolters (USA) [8]			
16. **J.Gimelstob** (USA) **& R.Wolters** (USA) [8]	...........6/4 4/6 6/4	...........6/1 6/1		
17. **D.De Melo** (BRA) **& R.Schlachter** (BRA) [5]	D.De Melo (BRA) & R.Schlachter (BRA) [5]			
18. D-H.Kim (KOR) & J-M.Lee (KOR)	...........7/6(1) 2/6 6/4	J-F.Bachelot (FRA) & R.Cadart (FRA)		
19. D.Bracciali (ITA) & D.Sciortino (ITA)	J-F.Bachelot (FRA) & R.Cadart (FRA)			
20. J-F.Bachelot (FRA) & R.Cadart (FRA)	...........6/3 4/6 6/4	...........6/1 6/4	T.Haas (GER) & G.Hill (USA) [3]	
21. P.Saurav (IND) & B.Witoonpanich (THA)	M.Russell (USA) & M.Tabara (CZE)			
22. M.Russell (USA) & M.Tabara (CZE)	...........6/0 6/4	T.Haas (GER) & G.Hill (USA) [3]	...........6/1 6/3	
23. J.Delgado (GBR) & A.Osterrieth (GBR)	T.Haas (GER) & G.Hill (USA) [3]			
24. **T.Haas** (GER) **& G.Hill** (USA) [3]	...........3/6 7/5 6/2	...........6/4 6/3		
25. **N.Kiefer** (GER) **& U-J.Seetzen** (GER) [6]	N.Kiefer (GER) & U-J.Seetzen (GER) [6]			
26. O.Mutis (FRA) & J.B.Perlant (FRA)	...........6/4 6/2	N.Kiefer (GER) & U-J.Seetzen (GER) [6]		
27. Y.Ishii (JPN) & N.Nash (AUS)	Y.Ishii (JPN) & N.Nash (AUS)			
28. R.Stepanek (CZE) & J.Vanek (CZE)	...........7/6(1) 7/6(10)	...........7/5 7/5	A.Hernandez (MEX) & M.Puerta (ARG) [2]	
29. S.Sidia (TUN) & V.Voltchkov (BLR)	D.Matijasevic (YUG) & V.Pavicevic (YUG)			
30. D.Matijasevic (YUG) & V.Pavicevic (YUG)	...........6/4 7/5	A.Hernandez (MEX) & M.Puerta (ARG) [2]	...........6/7(5) 6/2 6/3	
31. K.Bardoczky (HUN) & L.Vosloo (RSA)	A.Hernandez (MEX) & M.Puerta (ARG) [2]			
32. **A.Hernandez** (MEX) **& M.Puerta** (ARG) [2]	...........7/5 6/2	...........6/4 6/4		

Final: M.Lee (GBR) & J.M.Trotman (GBR) — 6/4 2/6 6/3 / 7/6(7) 6/4
A.Hernandez (MEX) & M.Puerta (ARG) [2] — 6/4 7/6(9)

Heavy type denotes seeded players. The encircled figure against names denotes the order in which they have been seeded.

The matches are the best of three sets

155

For both the Girls' Singles *and* the Girls' Doubles Championships, the winners become the holders, for one year only, of a cup presented by the All England Lawn Tennis and Croquet Club. The winners and runners-up each receive a personal prize.

Holder: Miss M. Hingis

First Round	Second Round	Third Round	Quarter-Finals	Semi-Finals	Final
1. **Miss Y.Basting [1]** ....(NED)	Miss Y.Basting [1]				
2. Miss O.Barabanschikova........(BLR)		Miss H.Inoue			
3. Miss H.Inoue ....(JPN)	Miss H.Inoue 7/5 6/4		Miss H.Inoue		
4. Miss R.Sandu ....(ROM)		6/4 6/4			
5. Miss F.E.Lishman ....(GBR)	Miss F.E.Lishman 6/4 6/1				
6. Miss M.Del Valle Prieto.........(MEX)		Miss L.Osterloh [13]	3/6 6/3 7/5		
7. Miss E.Chiew ....(MAL)	Miss L.Osterloh [13] 6/2 6/2	6/2 6/3		Miss H.Inoue	
8. **Miss L.Osterloh [13]** ....(USA)	6/1 6/2			4/6 7/5 6/4	
9. **Miss D.Chladkova [11]** ....(CZE)	Miss S.De Beer				
10. Miss S.De Beer	7/6(4) 6/2	Miss M.Weingartner			
11. Miss M.Weingartner ....(GER)	Miss M.Weingartner	6/3 6/3	Miss A.Castera		
12. Miss C.Black ....(ZIM)	6/3 1/6 6/3		7/6(4) 6/1		
13. Miss M.Vavrinec ....(SUI)		Miss A.Castera			
14. Miss A.Castera ....(FRA)	Miss A.Castera 6/2 7/5	6/3 6/3			
15. Miss D.Gaviria ....(PER)	Miss S.E.Drake Brockman [6]				
16. **Miss S.E.Drake Brockman [6]** ..(AUS)	6/1 6/2				Miss A.Olsza [9]
17. **Miss L.Varmuzova [4]** ....(SMR)	Miss L.Varmuzova [4]				6/2 7/5
18. Miss A.Basica ....(USA)	6/2 6/4	Miss L.Varmuzova [4]			
19. Miss P.Mandula ....(HUN)	Miss P.Mandula	6/4 6/4			
20. Miss K.Goldstein ....(MEX)	6/3 6/0		Miss A.Olsza [9]		
21. Miss M.Pastikova ....(CZE)	Miss M.Pastikova		4/6 7/5 3/0 retired		
22. Miss E.Roubanova ....(GBR)		Miss A.Olsza [9]			
23. Miss S.Nacuk ....(YUG)	Miss A.Olsza [9] 6/4 6/1	6/2 6/1		Miss A.Olsza [9]	
24. **Miss A.Olsza [9]** ....(POL)				6/2 6/3	
25. **Miss M.D'Agostini [15]** ....(BRA)	Miss T.Plivelitsch				
26. Miss T.Plivelitsch ....(GER)	6/1 6/2	Miss N.Dechy			
27. Miss N.Dechy ....(FRA)	Miss N.Dechy	7/5 4/6 6/2	Miss N.Dechy		
28. Miss S.Sfar ....(TUN)	6/4 6/3		6/2 7/6(5)		
29. Miss A.Venkatesan ....(AUS)	Miss S.Reeves				
30. Miss S.Reeves ....(USA)	6/3 7/6(4)	Miss T.Weng			
31. Miss T.Weng ....(TPE)	Miss T.Weng	6/2 7/6(5)			
32. Miss G.Swart ....(RSA)	6/7(5) 6/1 6/1				Miss A.Olsza [9]
33. **Miss T.Tanasugarn [5]** ....(THA)	Miss T.Tanasugarn [5]				7/5 7/6(6)
34. Miss W.Prakusya ....(INA)	6/3 6/2	Miss T.Tanasugarn [5]			
35. Miss C.Morariu ....(USA)	Miss C.Morariu	7/6(9) 1/1 retired			
36. Miss Z.Mellis ....(GBR)	6/2 6/1		Miss T.Tanasugarn [5]		
37. Miss L.Cervanova ....(SVK)		Miss L.Cervanova	6/4 6/4		
38. Miss A.Mauresmo ....(FRA)	Miss L.Cervanova 3/6 6/1 6/2	6/1 6/1			
39. Miss M.E.Rojas ....(PER)				Miss T.Tanasugarn [5]	
40. **Miss K.Nagy [12]** ....(HUN)	Miss K.Nagy [12] 6/3 6/4			6/4 6/3	
41. **Miss B.Schwartz [14]** ....(AUT)	Miss B.Schwartz [14]				
42. Miss S.Obata ....(JPN)	4/6 6/1 6/0	Miss B.Schwartz [14]			
43. Miss A.Monhartova ....(CZE)	Miss A.Monhartova	6/1 6/1			
44. Miss C-B.Khoo ....(MAL)	6/2 6/1		Miss B.Schwartz [14]		
45. Miss A.Tordoff ....(GBR)	Miss S.Klosel		7/6(6) 3/6 6/4		
46. Miss S.Klosel ....(GER)		Miss A.Ellwood [3]			
47. Miss A.Canepa ....(ITA)	Miss A.Ellwood [3] 6/4 6/2	6/2 6/1			
48. **Miss A.Ellwood [3]** ....(AUS)					Miss T.Tanasugarn [5]
49. **Miss A.Cocheteux [7]** ....(FRA)	Miss A.Cocheteux [7]				7/6(5) 6/3
50. Miss T.Poutchek ....(BLR)	2/6 7/6(2) 6/1	Miss S.Halsell			
51. Miss S.Halsell ....(USA)	Miss S.Halsell	1/6 7/5 6/2	Miss M.Jeon		
52. Miss K.Palme ....(MEX)			7/6(1) 6/2		
53. Miss P.Schnyder ....(SUI)	Miss M.Miller				
54. Miss M.Miller ....(GBR)	6/1 6/0	Miss M.Jeon			
55. Miss J.Steck ....(RSA)	Miss M.Jeon	6/2 6/4			
56. Miss M.Jeon ....(KOR)	6/3 6/4			Miss A.Kournikova [2]	
57. **Miss J.Schonfeldova [10]** .....(CZE)	Miss J.Schonfeldova [10]			6/3 1/6 6/4	
58. Miss W.L.Chan ....(HKG)	2/6 6/1 6/3	Miss T.Musgrave			
59. Miss K.Marosi ....(HUN)	Miss T.Musgrave	5/7 6/2 7/5	Miss A.Kournikova [2]		
60. Miss T.Musgrave ....(AUS)	6/1 6/2		7/6(2) 6/2		
61. Miss A.Pirsu ....(ROM)	Miss A.Pirsu				
62. Miss A.Radeljevic ....(CRO)	3/6 6/1 6/4	Miss A.Kournikova [2]			
63. Miss P.Hermida ....(ESP)	Miss A.Kournikova [2]	6/4 6/4			
64. **Miss A.Kournikova [2]** ....(RUS)	7/6(4) 7/5				

Holders: Miss E. De Villiers and Miss E.E. Jelfs

First Round	Second Round	Quarter-Finals	Semi-Finals	Final
1. **Miss C.Morariu** (USA) & **Miss L.Varmuzova** (SMR) ......[1]	Miss C.Morariu (USA) & Miss L.Varmuzova (SMR) [1]			
2. Miss M.Del Valle Prieto (MEX) & Miss M.E.Rojas (PER)	6/0 6/0	Miss C.Morariu (USA) & Miss L.Varmuzova (SMR) [1]		
3. Miss A.Kournikova (RUS) & Miss P.Mandula (HUN)	Miss A.Kournikova (RUS) & Miss P.Mandula (HUN)			
4. Miss T.Poutchek (BLR) & Miss S.Sfar (TUN)	4/6 6/1 6/4		Miss C.Morariu (USA) & Miss L.Varmuzova (SMR) [1]	
5. Miss M.Jeon (KOR) & Miss T.Tanasugarn (THA)	Miss K.Marosi (HUN) & Miss J.Steck (RSA)		6/4 5/7 6/4	
6. Miss K.Marosi (HUN) & Miss J.Steck (RSA)	1/6 6/4 6/4	Miss K.Marosi (HUN) & Miss J.Steck (RSA)		
7. Miss A.Pirsu (ROM) & Miss R.Sandu (ROM)	Miss A.Pirsu (ROM) & Miss R.Sandu (ROM)	6/0 6/1		
8. **Miss D.Gaviria** (PER) & **Miss P.Hermida** (ESP) ......[7]	6/1 6/0			Miss C.Black (ZIM) & Miss A.Olsza (POL) [3]
9. **Miss C.Black** (ZIM) & **Miss A.Olsza** (POL) ......[3]	Miss C.Black (ZIM) & Miss A.Olsza (POL) [3]			7/6(4) 6/4
10. Miss L.Cervanova (SVK) & Miss W.Prakusya (INA)	7/6(6) 6/3	Miss C.Black (ZIM) & Miss A.Olsza (POL) [3]		
11. Miss K.Goldstein (MEX) & Miss A.Radeljevic (CRO)	Miss K.Nagy (HUN) & Miss P.Schnyder (SUI)			
12. Miss K.Nagy (HUN) & Miss P.Schnyder (SUI)	6/4	6/2 2/6 6/2	Miss C.Black (ZIM) & Miss A.Olsza (POL) [3]	
13. Miss D.Chladkova (CZE) & Miss B.Schwartz (AUT)	Miss D.Chladkova (CZE) & Miss B.Schwartz (AUT)		3/6 6/1 6/2	
14. Miss M.Miller (GBR) & Miss A.Venkatesan (AUS)	6/0 6/2	Miss A.Cocheteux (FRA) & Miss A.Mauresmo (FRA) [8]		
15. Miss M.Pastikova (CZE) & Miss J.Schonfeldova (CZE)	Miss A.Cocheteux (FRA) & Miss A.Mauresmo (FRA) [8]	7/6 6/0		
16. **Miss A.Cocheteux** (FRA) & **Miss A.Mauresmo** (FRA) ......[8]	walk over			
17. Miss Y.Basting (NED) & Miss S.De Beer (RSA)	Miss F.Hearn (GBR) & Miss Z.Mellis (GBR)			
(W) 18. Miss F.Hearn (GBR) & Miss Z.Mellis (GBR)	walk over	Miss S.Halsell (USA) & Miss L.Osterloh (USA)		
19. Miss H.Inoue (JPN) & Miss S.Obata (JPN)	Miss S.Halsell (USA) & Miss L.Osterloh (USA)	6/4 6/0		
20. Miss S.Halsell (USA) & Miss L.Osterloh (USA)	6/2 6/0		Miss T.Musgrave (AUS) & Miss J.Richardson (AUS) [4]	
(W) 21. Miss F.E.Lishman (GBR) & Miss A.Tordoff (GBR)	Miss J.Choudhury (GBR) & Miss L.Ogan (GBR)		6/2 6/3	
22. Miss J.Choudhury (GBR) & Miss C.Ugan (GBR)	7/6(5) 6/2	Miss T.Musgrave (AUS) & Miss J.Richardson (AUS) [4]		
23. Miss T.Blackburn (GBR) & Miss C.Madden (RSA)	Miss T.Musgrave (AUS) & Miss J.Richardson (AUS) [4]	6/1 6/2		
24. **Miss T.Musgrave** (AUS) & **Miss J.Richardson** (AUS) ......[4]	6/1 6/0			Miss T.Musgrave (AUS) & Miss J.Richardson (AUS) [4]
25. **Miss S.E.Drake Brockman** (AUS) & **Miss A.Ellwood** (AUS) ......[5]	Miss S.E.Drake Brockman (AUS) & Miss A.Ellwood (AUS) [5]			6/0 7/6(5)
26. Miss L.Andriyani (INA) & Miss G.Swart (RSA)	7/5 6/3	Miss S.E.Drake Brockman (AUS) & Miss A.Ellwood (AUS) [5]		
27. Miss A.Castera (FRA) & Miss N.Dechy (FRA)	Miss A.Castera (FRA) & Miss N.Dechy (FRA)	6/3 2/6 6/2		
(W) 28. Miss L.Austin (GBR) & Miss E.Fletcher (GBR)	6/2 6/1		Miss A.Basica (USA) & Miss S.Reeves (USA)	
29. Miss A.Basica (USA) & Miss S.Reeves (USA)	Miss A.Basica (USA) & Miss S.Reeves (USA)		6/2 5/7 7/5	
30. Miss T.Callow (GBR) & Miss J.Osman (GBR)	6/3 6/1	Miss A.Basica (USA) & Miss S.Reeves (USA)		
31. Miss C-B.Khoo (MAL) & Miss T.Weng (TPE)	Miss O.Barabanschikova (BLR) & Miss A.Canepa (ITA) [2]	6/3 6/4		
32. **Miss O.Barabanschikova** (BLR) & **Miss A.Canepa** (ITA) ......[2]	6/4 6/4			

Heavy type denotes seeded players. The encircled figure against names denotes the order in which they have been seeded.

The matches are the best of three sets

Champions and Runners-up

1877 - S. W. Gore
W. C. Marshall

1878 - P. F. Hadow
S. W. Gore

* 1879 - J. T. Hartley
V. St. L. Goold

1880 - J. T. Hartley
H. F. Lawford

1881 - W. Renshaw
J. T. Hartley

1882 - W. Renshaw
E. Renshaw

1883 - W. Renshaw
E. Renshaw

1884 - W. Renshaw
H. F. Lawford

1885 - W. Renshaw
H. F. Lawford

1886 - W. Renshaw
H. F. Lawford

* 1887 - H. F. Lawford
E. Renshaw

1888 - E. Renshaw
H. F. Lawford

1889 - W. Renshaw
E. Renshaw

1890 - W. J. Hamilton
W. Renshaw

* 1891 - W. Baddeley
J. Pim

1892 - W. Baddeley
J. Pim

1893 - J. Pim
W. Baddeley

1894 - J. Pim
W. Baddeley

* 1895 - W. Baddeley
W. V. Eaves

1896 - H. S. Mahony
W. Baddeley

1897 - R. F. Doherty
H. S. Mahony

1898 - R. F. Doherty
H. L . Doherty

1899 - R. F. Doherty
A. W. Gore

1900 - R. F. Doherty
S. H. Smith

1901 - A. W. Gore
R. F. Doherty

1902 - H. L. Doherty
A. W. Gore

1903 - H. L. Doherty
F. L. Riseley

1904 - H. L. Doherty
F. L. Riseley

1905 - H. L. Doherty
N. E. Brookes

1906 - H. L. Doherty
F. L. Riseley

* 1907 - N. E. Brookes
A. W. Gore

* 1908 - A. W. Gore
H. Roper Barrett

1909 - A. W. Gore
M. J. G. Ritchie

1910 - A. F. Wilding
A. W. Gore

1911 - A. F. Wilding
H. Roper Barrett

1912 - A. F. Wilding
A. W. Gore

1913 - A. F. Wilding
M. E. McLoughlin

1914 - N. E. Brookes
A. F. Wilding

1919 - G. L. Patterson
N. E. Brookes

1920 - W. T. Tilden
G. L. Patterson

1921 - W. T. Tilden
B. I. C. Norton

*† 1922 - G. L. Patterson
R. Lycett

1923 - W. M. Johnston
F. T. Hunter

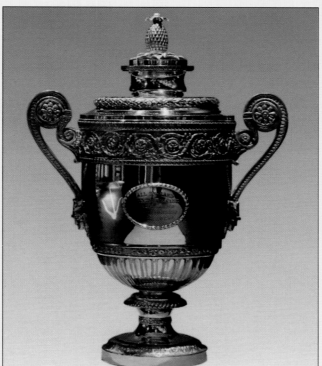

1924 - J. Borotra
R. Lacoste

1925 - R. Lacoste
J. Borotra

1926 - J. Borotra
H. Kinsey

1927 - H. Cochet
J. Borotra

1928 - R. Lacoste
H. Cochet

1929 - H. Cochet
J. Borotra

1930 - W. T. Tilden
W. Allison

1931 - S. B. Wood
F. X. Shields

1932 - H. E. Vines
H. W. Austin

1933 - J. H. Crawford
H. E. Vines

1934 - F. J. Perry
J. H. Crawford

1935 - F. J. Perry
G. von Cramm

1936 - F. J. Perry
G. von Cramm

* 1937 - J. D. Budge
G. von Cramm

1938 - J. D. Budge
H. W. Austin

* 1939 - R. L. Riggs
E. T. Cooke

* 1946 - Y. Petra
G. E. Brown

1947 - J. Kramer
T. Brown

* 1948 - R. Falkenburg
J. E. Bromwich

1949 - F. R. Schroeder
J. Drobny

* 1950 - B. Patty
F. A. Sedgman

1951 - R. Savitt
K. McGregor

1952 - F. A. Sedgman
J. Drobny

* 1953 - V. Seixas
K. Nielsen

1954 - J. Drobny
K. R. Rosewall

1955 - T. Trabert
K. Nielsen

* 1956 - L. A. Hoad
K. R. Rosewall

1957 - L. A. Hoad
A. J. Cooper

* 1958 - A. J. Cooper
N. A. Fraser

* 1959 - A. Olmedo
R. Laver

* 1960 - N. A. Fraser
R. Laver

1961 - R. Laver
C. R. McKinley

1962 - R. Laver
M. F. Mulligan

* 1963 - C. R. McKinley
F. S. Stolle

1964 - R. Emerson
F. S. Stolle

1965 - R. Emerson
F. S. Stolle

1966 - M. Santana
R. D. Ralston

1967 - J. D. Newcombe
W. P. Bungert

1968 - R. Laver
A. D. Roche

1969 - R. Laver
J. D. Newcombe

1970 - J. D. Newcombe
K. R. Rosewall

1971 - J. D. Newcombe
S. R. Smith

* 1972 - S. R. Smith
I. Nastase

* 1973 - J. Kodes
A. Metreveli

1974 - J. S. Connors
K. R. Rosewall

1975 - A. R. Ashe
J. S. Connors

1976 - B. Borg
I. Nastase

1977 - B. Borg
J. S. Connors

1978 - B. Borg
J. S.Connors

1979 - B. Borg
R. Tanner

1980 - B. Borg
J. P. McEnroe

1981 - J. P. McEnroe
B. Borg

1982 - J. S. Connors
J. P. McEnroe

1983 - J. P. McEnroe
C. J. Lewis

1984 - J. P. McEnroe
J. S. Connors

1985 - B. Becker
K. Curren

1986 - B.Becker
I. Lendl

1987 - P. Cash
I. Lendl

1988 - S. Edberg
B. Becker

1989 - B. Becker
S. Edberg

1990 - S. Edberg
B. Becker

1991 - M. Stich
B. Becker

1992 - A. Agassi
G. Ivanisevic

1993 - P. Sampras
J. Courier

1994 - P. Sampras
G. Ivanisevic

NOTE: For the years 1913, 1914 and 1919-23 inclusive the Championship Roll includes the 'World's Championship on Grass' granted to The Lawn Tennis Association by The International Lawn Tennis Federation. This title was then abolished and commencing in 1924 they became The Official Lawn Tennis Championships recognised by The International Lawn Tennis Federation.
Prior to 1922 the holders in the singles events and the gentlemen's doubles did not compete in The Championships but met the winners of these events in the Challenge Rounds.
† Challenge Round abolished; holders subsequently played through.   *The holder did not defend the title.

157

1884 - Miss M. Watson
Miss L. Watson

1885 - Miss M. Watson
Miss B. Bingley

1886 - Miss B. Bingley
Miss M. Watson

1887 - Miss L. Dod
Miss B. Bingley

1888 - Miss L. Dod
Mrs. G. W. Hillyard

* 1889 - Mrs. G. W. Hillyard
Miss L. Rice

* 1890 - Miss L. Rice
Miss M. Jacks

* 1891 - Miss L. Dod
Mrs. G. W. Hillyard

1892 - Miss L. Dod
Mrs. G. W. Hillyard

1893 - Miss L. Dod
Mrs. G. W. Hillyard

* 1894 - Mrs. G. W. Hillyard
Miss E. L. Austin

* 1895 - Miss C. Cooper
Miss H. Jackson

1896 - Miss C. Cooper
Mrs. W. H.Pickering

1897 - Mrs. G. W. Hillyard
Miss C. Cooper

* 1898 - Miss C. Cooper
Miss L Martin

1899 - Mrs. G. W. Hillyard
Miss C. Cooper

1900 - Mrs. G. W. Hillyard
Miss C. Cooper

1901 - Mrs. A. Sterry
Mrs. G. W. Hillyard

1902 - Miss M. E. Robb
Mrs. A. Sterry

* 1903 - Miss D. K. Douglass
Miss E. W. Thomson

1904 - Miss D. K. Douglass
Mrs. A. Sterry

1905 - Miss M. Sutton
Miss D. K. Douglass

1906 - Miss D. K Douglass
Miss M. Sutton

1907 - Miss M. Sutton
Mrs. Lambert Chambers

* 1908 - Mrs. A. Sterry
Miss A. M. Morton

* 1909 - Miss D. P. Boothby
Miss A. M. Morton

1910 - Mrs. Lambert Chambers
Miss D. P. Boothby

1911 - Mrs. Lambert Chambers
Miss D. P. Boothby

* 1912 - Mrs. D. R. Larcombe
Mrs. A. Sterry

* 1913 - Mrs. Lambert Chambers
Mrs. R. J. McNair

1914 - Mrs. Lambert Chambers
Mrs. D. R. Larcombe

1919 - Mlle. S. Lenglen
Mrs. Lambert Chambers

1920 - Mlle. S. Lenglen
Mrs. Lambert Chambers

1921 - Mlle. S. Lenglen
Miss E. Ryan

† 1922 - Mlle. S. Lenglen
Mrs. F. Mallory

1923 - Mlle. S. Lenglen
Miss K. McKane

1924 - Miss K. McKane
Miss H. Wills

1925 - Mlle. S. Lenglen
Miss J. Fry

1926 - Mrs. L. A. Godfree
Sta. L. de Alvarez

* 1927 - Miss H. Wills
Sta. L. de Alvarez

1928 - Miss H. Wills
Sta. L. de Alvarez

1929 - Miss H. Wills
Miss H. H. Jacobs

1930 - Mrs. F. S. Moody
Miss E. Ryan

* 1931 - Fraulein C. Aussem
Fraulein H. Krahwinkel

1932 - Mrs. F. S. Moody
Miss H. H. Jacobs

1933 - Mrs. F. S. Moody
Miss D. E. Round

* 1934 - Miss D. E. Round
Miss H. H. Jacobs

1935 - Mrs. F. S. Moody
Miss H. H. Jacobs

* 1936 - Miss H. H. Jacobs
Frau. S. Sperling

1937 - Miss D. E. Round
Miss J. Jedrzejowska

* 1938 - Mrs. F. S. Moody
Miss H. H. Jacobs

* 1939 - Miss A. Marble
Miss K. E. Stammers

* 1946 - Miss P. Betz
Miss L. Brough

* 1947 - Miss M. Osborne
Miss D. Hart

1948 - Miss L. Brough
Miss D. Hart

1949 - Miss L. Brough
Mrs. W. du Pont

1950 - Miss L. Brough
Mrs. W. du Pont

1951 - Miss D. Hart
Miss S. Fry

1952 - Miss M. Connolly
Miss L. Brough

1953 - Miss M. Connolly
Miss D. Hart

1954 - Miss M. Connolly
Miss L. Brough

* 1955 - Miss L. Brough
Mrs. J. G. Fleitz

1956 - Miss S. Fry
Miss A. Buxton

* 1957 - Miss A. Gibson
Miss D. R. Hard

1958 - Miss A. Gibson
Miss A. Mortimer

* 1959 - Miss M. E. Bueno
Miss D. R. Hard

1960 - Miss M. E. Bueno
Miss S. Reynolds

* 1961 - Miss A. Mortimer
Miss C. C. Truman

1962 - Mrs. J. R. Susman
Mrs. V. Sukova

* 1963 - Miss M. Smith
Miss B. J. Moffitt

1964 - Miss M. E. Bueno
Miss M. Smith

1965 - Miss M. Smith
Miss M. E. Bueno

1966 - Mrs. L. W. King
Miss M. E. Bueno

1967 - Mrs. L. W. King
Mrs. P. F. Jones

1968 - Mrs. L. W. King
Miss J. A. M. Tegart

1969 - Mrs. P. F. Jones
Mrs. L. W. King

* 1970 - Mrs. B. M. Court
Mrs. L. W. King

1971 - Miss E. F. Goolagong
Mrs. B. M. Court

1972 - Mrs. L. W. King
Miss E. F. Goolagong

1973 - Mrs. L. W. King
Miss C. M. Evert

1974 - Miss C. M. Evert
Mrs. O. Morozova

1975 - Mrs. L. W. King
Mrs. R. Cawley

* 1976 - Miss C. M. Evert
Mrs. R. Cawley

1977 - Miss S. V. Wade
Miss B. F. Stove

1978 - Miss M. Navratilova
Miss C. M. Evert

1979 - Miss M. Navratilova
Mrs. J. M. Lloyd

1980 - Mrs. R. Cawley
Mrs. J. M. Lloyd

1981 - Mrs. J. M. Lloyd
Miss H. Mandlikova

1982 - Miss M. Navratilova
Mrs. J. M. Lloyd

1983 - Miss M. Navratilova
Miss A. Jaeger

1984 - Miss M. Navratilova
Mrs. J. M. Lloyd

1985 - Miss M. Navratilova
Mrs. J. M. Lloyd

1986 - Miss M. Navratilova
Miss H. Mandlikova

1987 - Miss M. Navratilova
Miss S. Graf

1988 - Miss S. Graf
Miss M. Navratilova

1989 - Miss S. Graf
Miss M. Navratilova

1990 - Miss M. Navratilova
Miss Z. Garrison

1991 - Miss S. Graf
Miss G. Sabatini

1992 - Miss S. Graf
Miss M. Seles

1993 - Miss S. Graf
Miss J. Novotna

1994 - Miss C. Martinez
Miss M. Navratilova

MAIDEN NAMES OF LADY CHAMPIONS
In the tables the following have been recorded
in both married and single identities.

Mrs. R. Cawley	Miss E. F. Goolagong		Mrs. F. S. Moody	Miss H. Wills
Mrs. Lambert Chambers	Miss D. K. Douglass		Mrs. O. Morozova	Miss O. Morozova
Mrs. B. M. Court	Miss M. Smith	Mrs. G. W. Hillyard	Miss B. Bingley	Mrs. L. E. G. Price	Miss S. Reynolds
Mrs. B. C. Covell	Miss P. L. Howkins	Mrs. P. F. Jones	Miss A. S. Haydon	Mrs. G. E. Reid	Miss K. Melville
Mrs. D. E. Dalton	Miss J. A. M. Tegart	Mrs. L. W. King	Miss B. J. Moffitt	Mrs. P. D. Smylie	Miss E. M. Sayers
Mrs. W. du Pont	Miss M. Osborne	Mrs. M. R. King	Miss P. E. Mudford	Frau. S. Sperling	Fraulein H. Krahwinkel
Mrs. L. A. Godfree	Miss K. McKane	Mrs. D. R. Larcombe	Miss E. W. Thomson	Mrs. A. Sterry	Miss C. Cooper
Mrs. H. F. Gourlay Cawley	Miss H. F. Gourlay	Mrs. J. M. Lloyd	Miss C. M. Evert	Mrs. J. R. Susman	Miss K. Hantze

MEN'S DOUBLES

1879 - L. R. Erskine and H. F. Lawford
F. Durant and G. E. Tabor
1880 - W. Renshaw and E. Renshaw
O. E. Woodhouse and C. J. Cole
1881 - W. Renshaw and E. Renshaw
W. J. Down and H. Vaughan
1882 - J. T. Hartley and R. T. Richardson
J. G. Horn and C. B. Russell
1883 - C. W. Grinstead and C. E. Welldon
C. B. Russell and R. T. Milford
1884 - W. Renshaw and E. Renshaw
E. W. Lewis and E.L Williams
1885 - W. Renshaw and E. Renshaw
C. E. Farrer and A. J. Stanley
1886 - W. Renshaw and E. Renshaw
C. E. Farrer and A. J. Stanley
1887 - P. Bowes-Lyon and H. W. W. Wilberforce
J. H. Crispe and E. Barratt Smith
1888 - W. Renshaw and E. Renshaw
P Bowes-Lyon and H. W. W. Wilberforce
1889 - W. Renshaw and E. Renshaw
E. W. Lewis and G. W. Hillyard
1890 - J. Pim and F. O. Stoker
E. W. Lewis and G. W. Hillyard
1891 - W. Baddeley and H. Baddeley
J. Pim and F. O. Stoker
1892 - H. S. Barlow and E. W. Lewis
W. Baddeley and H. Baddeley
1893 - J. Pim and F. O. Stoker
E. W. Lewis and H. S. Barlow
1894 - W. Baddeley and H. Baddeley
H. S. Barlow and C. H. Martin
1895 - W. Baddeley and H. Baddeley
E. W. Lewis and W. V. Eaves
1896 - W. Baddeley and H. Baddeley
R. F. Doherty and H. A. Nisbet
1897 - R. F. Doherty and H. L. Doherty
W. Baddeley and H. Baddeley
1898 - R. F. Doherty and H. L . Doherty
H. A. Nisbet and C. Hobart
1899 - R. F. Doherty and H. L. Doherty
H. A. Nisbet and C. Hobart
1900 - R. F. Doherty and H. L. Doherty
H. Roper Barrett and H. A. Nisbet
1901 - R. F. Doherty and H. L. Doherty
Dwight Davis and Holcombe Ward
1902 - S. H. Smith and F. L. Riseley
R. F. Doherty and H. L. Doherty
1903 - R. F. Doherty and H. L. Doherty
S. H. Smith and F. L. Riseley
1904 - R. F. Doherty and H. L. Doherty
S. H. Smith and F. L. Riseley
1905 - R. F. Doherty and H. L. Doherty
S. H. Smith and F. L. Riseley
1906 - S. H. Smith and F. L. Riseley
R. F. Doherty and H. L. Doherty
1907 - N. E. Brooks and A. F. Wilding
B. C. Wright and K. H. Behr
1908 - A. F. Wilding and M. J. G. Ritchie
A. W. Gore and H. Roper Barrett
1909 - A. W. Gore and H. Roper Barrett
S. N. Doust and H. A. Parker
1910 - A. F. Wilding and M. J. G. Ritchie
A. W. Gore and H. Roper Barrett
1911 - M. Decugis and A. H. Gobert
M. J. G. Ritchie and A. F. Wilding
1912 - H. Roper Barrett and C. P. Dixon
M. Decugis and A. H. Gobert
1913 - H. Roper Barrett and C. P. Dixon
F. W. Rahe and H. Kleinschroth
1914 - N. E. Brookes and A. F. Wilding
H. Roper Barrett and C. P. Dixon
1919 - R. V. Thomas and P. O'Hara-Wood
R. Lycett and R. W. Heath
1920 - R. N. Williams and C. S. Garland
A. R. F. Kingscote and J. C. Parke
1921 - R. Lycett and M. Woosnam
F. G. Lowe and A. H. Lowe
1922 - R. Lycett and J. O. Anderson
G. L. Patterson and P. O'Hara-Wood
1923 - R. Lycett and L. A. Godfree
Count de Gomar and E. Flaquer
1924 - F. T. Hunter and V. Richards
R. N. Williams and W. M. Washburn
1925 - J. Borotra and R. Lacoste
J. Hennessey and R. Casey
1926 - H. Cochet and J. Brugnon
V. Richards and H. Kinsey
1927 - F. T. Hunter and W. T. Tilden
J. Brugnon and H. Cochet
1928 - H. Cochet and J. Brugnon
G. L. Patterson and J. B. Hawkes
1929 - W. Allison and J. Van Ryn
J. C. Gregory and I. G. Collins
1930 - W. Allison and J. Van Ryn
J. H. Doeg and G. M. Lott
1931 - G. M Lott and J. Van Ryn
H. Cochet and J. Brugnon
1932 - J. Borotra and J. Brugnon
G. P. Hughes and F. J. Perry
1933 - J. Borotra and J. Brugnon
R. Nunoi and J. Satoh
1934 - G. M. Lott and L. R. Stoefen
J. Borotra and J. Brugnon
1935 - J. H. Crawford and A. K . Quist
W. Allison and J. Van Ryn
1936 - G. P. Hughes and C. R. D. Tuckey
C. E. Hare and F. H. D. Wilde
1937 - J. D. Budge and G. Mako
G. P. Hughes and C. R. D. Tuckey
1938 - J. D. Budge and G. Mako
H. Henkel and G. von Metaxa
1939 - R. L. Riggs and E. T. Cooke
C. E. Hare and F. H. D. Wilde
1946 - T. Brown and J. Kramer
G. E. Brown and D. Pails
1947 - R. Falkenburg and J. Kramer
A. J. Mottram and O. W. Sidwell
1948 - J. E. Bromwich and F. A. Sedgman
T. Brown and G. Mulloy
1949 - R. Gonzales and F. Parker
G. Mulloy and F. R. Schroeder
1950 - J. E. Bromwich and A. K. Quist
G. E. Brown and O. W Sidwell
1951 - K. McGregor and F. A. Sedgman
J. Drobny and E. W. Sturgess
1952 - K. McGregor and F. A. Sedgman
V. Seixas and E. W. Sturgess
1953 - L. A. Hoad and K. R. Rosewall
R. N. Hartwig and M. G. Rose
1954 - R. N. Hartwig and M. G. Rose
V. Seixas and T. Trabert
1955 - R. N. Hartwig and L. A. Hoad
N. A. Fraser and K. R. Rosewall
1956 - L. A. Hoad and K. R. Rosewall
N. Pietrangeli and O. Sirola
1957 - G. Mulloy and B. Patty
N. A. Fraser and L. A. Hoad
1958 - S. Davidson and U. Schmidt
A. J. Cooper and N. A. Fraser
1959 - R. Emerson and N. A. Fraser
R. Laver and R. Mark
1960 - R. H. Osuna and R. D. Ralston
M. G. Davies and R. K. Wilson
1961 - R. Emerson and N. A. Fraser
R. A. J. Hewitt and F. S. Stolle
1962 - R. A. J. Hewitt and F. S. Stolle
B. Jovanovic and N. Pilic
1963 - R. H. Osuna and A. Palafox
J. C. Barclay and P. Darmon
1964 - R. A. J. Hewitt and F. S. Stolle
R. Emerson and K. N. Fletcher
1965 - J. D. Newcombe and A. D. Roche
K. N. Fletcher and R. A. J. Hewitt
1966 - K. N. Fletcher and J. D. Newcombe
W. W. Bowrey and O. K. Davidson
1967 - R. A. J. Hewitt and F. D. McMillan
R. Emerson and K. N. Fletcher
1968 - J. D. Newcombe and A. D. Roche
K. R. Rosewall and F. S. Stolle
1969 - J. D. Newcombe and A. D. Roche
T. S. Okker and M. C. Reissen
1970 - J. D. Newcombe and A. D. Roche
K. R. Rosewall and F. S. Stolle
1971 - R. S. Emerson and R. G. Laver
A. R. Ashe and R. D. Ralston
1972 - R. A. J. Hewitt and F. D. McMillan
S. R. Smith and E. J. van Dillen
1973 - J. S. Connors and I. Nastase
J. R. Cooper and N. A. Fraser
1974 - J. D. Newcombe and A. D. Roche
R. C. Lutz and S. R. Smith
1975 - V. Gerulaitis and A. Mayer
C. Dowdeswell and A. J. Stone
1976 - B. E. Gottfried and R. Ramirez
R. L. Case and G. Masters
1977 - R. L. Case and G. Masters
J. G. Alexander and P. C. Dent
1978 - R. A. J. Hewitt and F. D. McMillan
P. Fleming and J. P. McEnroe
1979 - P. Fleming and J. P . McEnroe
B. E. Gottfried and R. Ramirez
1980 - P. McNamara and P. McNamee
R. C. Lutz and S. R. Smith
1981 - P. Fleming and J. P. McEnroe
R. C. Lutz and S. R. Smith
1982 - P. McNamara and P. McNamee
P. Fleming and J. P. McEnroe
1983 - P. Fleming and J. P McEnroe
T. E. Gullikson and T. R. Gullikson
1984 - P. Fleming and J. P. McEnroe
P. Cash and P. McNamee
1985 - H. P. Guenthardt and B. Taroczy
P. Cash and J. B. Fitzgerald
1986 - J. Nystrom and M. Wilander
G. Donnelly and P. Fleming
1987 - K. Flach and R. Seguso
S. Casal and E. Sanchez
1988 - K. Flach and R. Seguso
J. B. Fitzgerald and A. Jarryd
1889 - J. B. Fitzgerald and A. Jarryd
R. Leach and J. Pugh
1990 - R. Leach and J. Pugh
P. Aldrich and D. T. Visser
1991 - J. B. Fitzgerald and A. Jarryd
J. Frana and L. Lavalle
1992 - J. P. McEnroe and M. Stich
J. Grabb and R. A. Reneberg
1993 - T. A. Woodbridge and M. Woodforde
G. Connell and P. Galbraith
1994 - T. A. Woodbridge and M. Woodforde
G. Connell and P. Galbraith

LADIES' DOUBLES

1913 - Mrs. R. J. McNair and Miss D. P. Boothby
Mrs. A. Sterry and Mrs. Lambert Chambers
1914 - Miss E. Ryan and Miss A. M. Morton
Mrs. D. R. Larcombe and Mrs. F. J. Hannam
1919 - Mlle. S. Lenglen and Miss E. Ryan
Mrs. Lambert Chambers and Mrs. D. R. Larcombe
1920 - Mlle. S. Lenglen and Miss E. Ryan
Mrs. Lambert Chambers and Mrs. D. R. Larcombe
1921 - Mlle. S. Lenglen and Miss E. Ryan
Mrs. A. E. Beamish and Mrs. G. E. Peacock
1922 - Mlle. S. Lenglen and Miss E. Ryan
Mrs. A. D. Stocks and Miss K. McKane
1923 - Mlle. S. Lenglen and Miss E. Ryan
Miss J. Austin and Miss E. L. Colyer
1924 - Mrs. H. Wightman and Miss H. Wills
Mrs. B. C. Covell and Miss K. McKane
1925 - Mlle. S. Lenglen and Miss E. Ryan
Mrs. A. V. Bridge and Mrs. C. G. McIlquham
1926 - Miss E. Ryan and Miss M. K. Browne
Mrs. L. A. Godfree and Miss E. L. Colyer
1927 - Miss H. Wills and Miss E. Ryan
Miss E. L. Heine and Mrs. G. E. Peacock
1928 - Mrs. Holcroft-Watson and Miss P. Saunders
Miss E. H. Harvey and Miss E. Bennett
1929 - Mrs. Holcroft-Watson and Mrs. L. R. C. Michell
Mrs. B. C. Covell and Mrs. D. C. Shepherd-Barron
1930 - Mrs. F. S. Moody and Miss E. Ryan
Miss E. Cross and Miss S. Palfrey
1931 - Mrs. D. C. Shepherd-Barron and Miss P. E. Mudford
Mlle. D. Metaxa and Mlle. J. Sigart
1932 - Mlle. D. Metaxa and Mlle. J. Sigart
Miss E. Ryan and Miss H. H. Jacobs
1933 - Mme. R. Mathieu and Miss E. Ryan
Miss F. James and Miss A. M. Yorke
1934 - Mme. R. Mathieu and Miss E. Ryan
Mrs. D. Andrus and Mme. S. Henrotin
1935 - Miss F. James and Miss K. E. Stammers
Mme. R. Mathieu and Frau. S. Sperling
1936 - Miss F. James and Miss K. E. Stammers
Mrs. S. P. Fabyan and Miss H. H. Jacobs
1937 - Mme. R. Mathieu and Miss A. M. Yorke
Mrs. M. R. King and Mrs. J. B. Pittman
1938 - Mrs. S. P. Fabyan and Miss A. Marble
Mme. R. Mathieu and Miss A. M. Yorke
1939 - Mrs S. P. Fabyan and Miss A. Marble
Miss H. H. Jacobs and Miss A. M. Yorke
1946 - Miss L. Brough and Miss M. Osborne
Miss P. Betz and Miss D. Hart
1947 - Miss D. Hart and Mrs. P. C. Todd
Miss L. Brough and Miss M. Osborne
1948 - Miss L. Brough and Mrs. W. du Pont
Miss D. Hart and Mrs. P. C. Todd
1949 - Miss L. Brough and Mrs. W. du Pont
Miss G. Moran and Mrs. P. C. Todd
1950 - Miss L. Brough and Mrs. W. du Pont
Miss S. Fry and Miss D. Hart
1951 - Miss S. Fry and Miss D. Hart
Miss L. Brough and Mrs. W. du Pont
1952 - Miss S. Fry and Miss D. Hart
Miss L. Brough and Miss M. Connolly
1953 - Miss S. Fry and Miss D. Hart
Miss M. Connolly and Miss J. Sampson
1954 - Miss L. Brough and Mrs. W. du Pont
Miss S. Fry and Miss D. Hart
1955 - Miss A. Mortimer and Miss J. A. Shilcock
Miss S. J. Bloomer and Miss P. E. Ward
1956 - Miss A. Buxton and Miss A. Gibson
Miss F. Muller and Miss D. G. Seeney
1957 - Miss A. Gibson and Miss D. R. Hard
Mrs. K. Hawton and Mrs. T. D. Long
1958 - Miss M. E. Bueno and Miss A. Gibson
Mrs. W. du Pont and Miss M. Varner
1959 - Miss J. Arth and Miss D. R. Hard
Mrs. J. G. Fleitz and Miss C. C. Truman
1960 - Miss M. E. Bueno and Miss D. R. Hard
Miss S. Reynolds and Miss R. Schuurman
1961 - Miss K. Hantze and Miss B. J. Moffitt
Miss J. Lehane and Miss M. Smith
1962 - Miss B. J. Moffitt and Mrs. J. R. Susman
Mrs. L. E. G. Price and Miss R. Schuurman
1963 - Miss M. E. Bueno and Miss D. R. Hard
Miss R. A. Ebbern and Miss M. Smith
1964 - Miss M. Smith and Miss L. R. Turner
Miss B. J. Moffitt and Mrs. J. R. Susman
1965 - Miss M. E. Bueno and Miss B. J. Moffitt
Miss F. Durr and Miss J. Lieffrig
1966 - Miss M. E. Bueno and Miss N. Richey
Miss M. Smith and Miss J. A. M. Tegart
1967 - Miss R. Casals and Mrs. L. W. King
Miss M. E. Bueno and Miss N. Richey
1968 - Miss R. Casals and Mrs. L. W. King
Miss F. Durr and Mrs. P. F. Jones
1969 - Mrs. B. M. Court and Miss J. A. M. Tegart
Miss P. S. A. Hogan and Miss M. Michel
1970 - Miss R. Casals and Mrs. L. W. King
Miss F. Durr and Miss S. V. Wade
1971 - Miss R. Casals and Mrs. L. W. King
Mrs. B. M. Court and Miss E. F. Goolagong
1972 - Mrs. L. W. King and Miss B. F. Stove
Mrs. D. E. Dalton and Miss F. Durr
1973 - Miss R. Casals and Mrs. L. W. King
Miss F. Durr and Miss B. F. Stove
1974 - Miss E. F. Goolagong and Miss M. Michel
Miss H. F. Gourlay and Miss K. M. Krantzcke
1975 - Miss A. Kiyomura and Miss K. Sawamatsu
Miss F. Durr and Miss B. F. Stove
1976 - Miss C. M. Evert and Miss M. Navratilova
Mrs. L. W. King and Miss B. F. Stove
1977 - Mrs. H. F. Gourlay Cawley and Miss J. C. Russell
Miss M. Navratilova and Miss B. F . Stove
1978 - Mrs. G. E. Reid and Miss. W. M. Turnbull
Miss M. Jausovec and Miss V. Ruzici
1979 - Mrs. L. W. King and Miss M. Navratilova
Miss B. F. Stove and Miss W. M. Turnbull
1980 - Miss K. Jordan and Miss A. E. Smith
Miss R. Casals and Miss W. M. Turnbull
1981 - Miss M. Navratilova and Miss P. H. Shriver
Miss K. Jordan and Miss A. E. Smith
1982 - Miss M. Navratilova and Miss P. H. Shriver
Miss K. Jordan and Miss A. E. Smith
1983 - Miss M. Navratilova and Miss P. H. Shriver
Miss R. Casals and Miss W. M. Turnbull
1984 - Miss M. Navratilova and Miss P. H. Shriver
Miss K. Jordan and Miss A. E. Smith
1985 - Miss K. Jordan and Mrs. P. D. Smylie
Miss M. Navratilova and Miss P. H. Shriver
1986 - Miss M. Navratilova and Miss P. H. Shriver
Miss H. Mandlikova and Miss W. M. Turnbull
1987 - Miss C. Kohde-Kilsch and Miss H. Sukova
Miss B. Nagelsen and Mrs. P. D. Smylie
1988 - Miss S. Graf and Miss G. Sabatini
Miss L. Savchenko and Miss N. Zvereva
1989 - Miss J. Novotna and Miss H. Sukova
Miss L. Savchenko and Miss N. Zvereva
1990 - Miss J. Novotna and Miss H. Sukova
Miss K. Jordan and Mrs. P. D. Smylie
1991 - Miss L. Savchenko and Miss N. Zvereva
Miss G. Fernandez and Miss J. Novotna
1992 - Miss G. Fernandez and Miss N. Zvereva
Miss J. Novotna and Mrs. L. Savchenko-Neiland
1993 - Miss G. Fernandez and Miss N. Zvereva
Mrs. L. Neiland and Miss J. Novotna
1994 - Miss G. Fernandez and Miss N. Zvereva
Miss J. Novotna and Miss A. Sanchez Vicario

MIXED DOUBLES

1913 - Hope Crisp and Mrs. C. O. Tuckey J. C. Parke and Mrs. D. R. Larcombe	1947 - J. E. Bromwich and Miss L. Brough C. F. Long and Mrs. N. M. Bolton	1971 - O. K. Davidson and Mrs. L. W. King M. C. Riessen and Mrs. B. M. Court
1914 - J. C. Parke and Mrs. D.R. Larcombe A. F. Wilding and Mlle. M. Broquedis	1948 - J. E. Bromwich and Miss L. Brough F. A. Sedgman and Miss D. Hart	1972 - I. Nastase and Miss R. Casals K.G. Warwick and Miss E. F. Goolagong
1919 - R. Lycett and Miss E. Ryan A. D. Prebble and Mrs. Lambert Chambers	1949 - E. W. Sturgess and Mrs. S. P. Summers J. E. Bromwich and Miss L. Brough	1973 - O. K. Davidson and Mrs. L. W. King R. Ramirez and J. S. Newberry
1920 - G. L. Patterson and Mlle. S. Lenglen R. Lycett and Miss E. Ryan	1950 - E. W. Sturgess and Miss L. Brough G. E. Brown and Mrs. P. C. Todd	1974 - O. K. Davidson and Mrs. L. W. King M. J. Farrell and Miss L. J. Charles
1921 - R. Lycett and Miss E. Ryan M. Woosnam and Miss P. L. Howkins	1951 - F. A. Sedgman and Miss D. Hart M. G. Rose and Mrs. N. M. Bolton	1975 - M. C. Riessen and Mrs. B. M. Court A. J. Stone and Miss B. F. Stove
1922 - P. O'Hara-Wood and Mlle. S. Lenglen R. Lycett and Miss E. Ryan	1952 - F. A. Sedgman and Miss D. Hart E. Morea and Mrs. T. D. Long	1976 - A. D. Roche and Miss F. Durr R. L. Stockton and Miss R. Casals
1923 - R. Lycett and Miss E. Ryan L. S. Deane and Mrs. D. C. Shepherd-Barron	1953 - V. Seixas and Miss D. Hart E. Morea and Miss S. Fry	1977 - R. A. J. Hewitt and Miss G. R. Stevens F. D. McMillan and Miss B. F. Stove
1924 - J. B. Gilbert and Miss K. McKane L. A. Godfree and Mrs. D. C. Shepherd-Barron	1954 - V. Seixas and Miss D. Hart K. R. Rosewall and Mrs. W. du Pont	1978 - F. D. McMillan and Miss B. F. Stove R. O. Ruffels and Miss L. W. King
1925 - J. Borotra and Mlle. S. Lenglen H. L. de Morpurgo and Miss E. Ryan	1955 - V. Seixas and Miss D. Hart E. Morea and Miss L. Brough	1979 - R. A. J. Hewitt and Miss G. R. Stevens F. D. McMillan and Miss B. F. Stove
1926 - L. A. Godfree and Mrs. L. A. Godfree H. Kinsey and Miss M. K. Browne	1956 - V. Seixas and Miss S. Fry G. Mulloy and Miss A. Gibson	1980 - J. R. Austin and Miss T. Austin M. R. Edmondson and Miss D. L. Fromholtz
1927 - F. T. Hunter and Miss E. Ryan L. A. Godfree and Miss L. A. Godfree	1957 - M. G. Rose and Miss D. R. Hard N. A. Fraser and Miss A. Gibson	1981 - F. D. McMillan and Miss B. F. Stove J. R. Austin and Miss T. Austin
1928 - P. D. B. Spence and Miss E. Ryan J. Crawford and Miss D. Akhurst	1958 - R. N. Howe and Miss L. Coghlan K. Nielsen and Miss A. Gibson	1982 - K. Curren and Miss A. E. Smith J. M. Lloyd and Miss W. M. Turnbull
1929 - F. T. Hunter and Miss H. Wills I. G. Collins and Miss J. Fry	1959 - R. Laver and Miss D. R. Hard N. A. Fraser and Miss M. E. Bueno	1983 - J. M. Lloyd and Miss W. M. Turnbull S. Denton and Mrs. L. W. King
1930 - J. H. Crawford and Miss E. Ryan D. Prenn and Fraulein H. Krahwinkel	1960 - R. Laver and Miss D. R. Hard R. N. Howe and Miss M. E. Bueno	1984 - J. M. Lloyd and Miss W. M. Turnbull S. Denton and Miss K. Jordan
1931 - G. M. Lott and Mrs L. A. Harper I. G. Collins and Miss J. C. Ridley	1961 - F. S. Stolle and Miss L. R. Turner R. N. Howe and Miss E. Buding	1985 - P. McNamee and Miss M. Navratilova J. B. Fitzgerald and Mrs. P. D. Smylie
1932 - E. Maier and Miss E. Ryan H. C. Hopman and Mlle. J. Sigart	1962 - N. A. Fraser and Mrs. W. du Pont R. D. Ralston and Miss A. S. Haydon	1986 - K. Flach and Miss K. Jordan H. P. Guenthardt and Miss M. Navratilova
1933 - G. von Cramm and Fraulein H. Krahwinkel N. G. Farquharson and Miss M. Heeley	1963 - K. N. Fletcher and Miss M. Smith R. A. J. Hewitt and Miss D. R. Hard	1987 - M. J. Bates and Miss J. M. Durie D. Cahill and Miss N. Provis
1934 - R. Miki and Miss D. E. Round H. W. Austin and Mrs D. C. Shepherd-Barron	1964 - F. S. Stolle and Miss L. R. Turner K. N. Fletcher and Miss M. Smith	1988 - S. E. Stewart and Miss Z. L. Garrison K. Jones and Mrs. S. W. Magers
1935 - F. J. Perry and Miss D. E. Round H. C. Hopman and Mrs. H. C. Hopman	1965 - K. N. Fletcher and Miss M. Smith A. D. Roche and Miss J. A. M. Tegart	1989 - J. Pugh and Miss J. Novotna M. Kratzmann and Miss J. M. Byrne
1936 - F. J. Perry and Miss D. E. Round J. D. Budge and Mrs. S. P. Fabyan	1966 - K. N. Fletcher and Miss M. Smith R. D. Ralston and Mrs. L. W. King	1990 - R. Leach and Miss Z. L. Garrison J. B. Fitzgerald and Mrs P. D. Smylie
1937 - J. D. Budge and Miss A. Marble Y. Petra and Mme. R. Mathieu	1967 - O. K. Davidson and Mrs. L. W. King K. N. Fletcher and Miss M. E. Bueno	1991 - J. B. Fitzgerald and Mrs. P. D. Smylie J. Pugh and Miss N. Zvereva
1938 - J. D. Budge and Miss A. Marble H. Henkel and Mrs. S. P. Fabyan	1968 - K. N. Fletcher and Mrs. B. M. Court A. Metreveli and Miss O. Morozova	1992 - C. Suk and Mrs L. Savchenko-Neiland J. Eltingh and Miss M. Oremans
1939 - R. L. Riggs and Miss A. Marble F. H. D. Wilde and Miss N. B. Brown	1969 - F. S. Stolle and Miss P. F. Jones A. D. Roche and Miss J. A. M. Tegart	1993 - M. Woodforde and Miss M. Navratilova T. Nijssen and Miss M. M. Bollegraf
1946 - T. Brown and Miss L. Brough G. E. Brown and Miss D. Bundy	1970 - I. Nastase and Miss R. Casals A. Metreveli and Miss O. Morozova	1994 - T. A. Woodbridge and Miss H. Sukova T. J. Middleton and Miss L. M. McNeil

THE JUNIOR CHAMPIONSHIP ROLL

BOYS' SINGLES

1947 - K. Nielsen (Denmark)	1959 - T. Lejus (U.S.S.R.)	1971 - R. Kreiss (U.S.A.)	1983 - S. Edberg (Sweden)
1948 - S. Stockenberg (Sweden)	1960 - A. R. Mandelstam (S.A.)	1972 - B. Borg (Sweden)	1984 - M.Kratzmann (Australia)
1949 - S. Stockenberg (Sweden)	1961 - C. E. Graebner (U.S.A.)	1973 - W. Martin (U.S.A.)	1985 - L. Lavalle (Mexico)
1950 - J. A.T. Horn (G.B.)	1962 - S. Matthews (G.B.)	1974 - W. Martin (U.S.A.)	1986 - E. Velez (Mexico)
1951 - J. Kupferburger (S.A.)	1963 - N. Kalogeropoulos (Greece)	1975 - C. J. Lewis (N.Z.)	1987 - D. Nargiso (Italy)
1952 - R. K. Wilson (G.B.)	1964 - I. El Shafei (U.A.R.)	1976 - H. Guenthardt (Switzerland)	1988 - N. Pereira (Venezuela)
1953 - W. A. Knight (G.B.)	1965 - V. Korotkov (U.S.S.R.)	1977 - V. A. Winitsky (U.S.A.)	1989 - N. Kulti (Sweden)
1954 - R. Krishnan (India)	1966 - V. Korotkov (U.S.S.R.)	1978 - I. Lendl (Czechoslovakia)	1990 - L. Paes (India)
1955 - M. P. Hann (G.B.)	1967 - M. Orantes (Spain)	1979 - R. Krishnan (India)	1991 - T. Enquist (Sweden)
1956 - R. Holmberg (U.S.A.)	1968 - J. G. Alexander (Australia)	1980 - T. Tulasne (France)	1992 - D. Skoch (Czechoslovakia)
1957 - J. I. Tattersall (G.B.)	1969 - B. Bertram (S.A.)	1981 - M. W. Anger (U.S.A.)	1993 - R. Sabau (Romania)
1958 - E. Buchholz (U.S.A.)	1970 - B. Bertram (S.A.)	1982 - P. Cash (Australia)	1994 - S. Humphries (U.S.A.)

BOYS' DOUBLES

1982 - P. Cash and J. Frawley	1987 - J. Stoltenberg and T. Woodbridge	1992 - S. Baldas and S. Draper
1983 - M. Kratzmann and S. Youl	1988 - J. Stoltenberg and T. Woodbridge	1993 - S. Downs and J. Greenhalgh
1984 - R. Brown and R. Weiss	1989 - J. Palmer and J. Stark	1994 - B. Ellwood and M. Philippoussis
1985 - A. Moreno and J. Yzaga	1990 - S. Lareau and S. Leblanc	
1986 - T. Carbonell and P. Korda	1991 - K. Alami and G. Rusedski	

GIRLS' SINGLES

1948 - Miss O. Miskova (Czechoslovakia)	1960 - Miss K. Hantze (U.S.A.)	1972 - Miss I. Kloss (S.A.)	1984 - Miss A. N. Croft (G.B.)
1949 - Miss C. Mercelis (Belgium)	1961 - Miss G. Baksheeva (U.S.S.R.)	1973 - Miss A. Kiyomura (U.S.A.)	1985 - Miss A. Holikova (Czechoslovakia)
1950 - Miss L. Cornell (G.B.)	1962 - Miss G. Baksheeva (U.S.S.R.)	1974 - Miss M. Jausovec (Yugoslavia)	1986 - Miss N. Zvereva (U.S.S.R.)
1951 - Miss L. Cornell (G.B.)	1963 - Miss D. M. Salfati (France)	1975 - Miss N. Y. Chmyreva (U.S.S.R.)	1987 - Miss N. Zvereva (U.S.S.R.)
1952 - Miss ten Bosch (Netherlands)	1964 - Miss P. Bartkowicz (U.S.A.)	1976 - Miss N. Y. Chmyreva (U.S.S.R.)	1988 - Miss B. Schultz (Netherlands)
1953 - Miss D. Kilian (S.A.)	1965 - Miss O. Morozova (U.S.S.R.)	1977 - Miss L. Antonoplis (U.S.A.)	1989 - Miss A. Strnadova (Czechoslovakia)
1954 - Miss V. A. Pitt (G.B.)	1966 - Miss B. Lindstrom (Finland)	1978 - Miss T. Austin (U.S.A.)	1990 - Miss A. Strnadova (Czechoslovakia)
1955 - Miss S. M. Armstrong (G.B.)	1967 - Miss J. Salome (Netherlands)	1979 - Miss M. L. Piatek (U.S.A.)	1991 - Miss B. Rittner (Germany)
1956 - Miss A. S. Haydon (G.B.)	1968 - Miss K. Pigeon (U.S.A.)	1980 - Miss D. Freeman (Australia)	1992 - Miss C. Rubin (U.S.A.)
1957 - Miss M. Arnold (U.S.A.)	1969 - Miss K. Sawamatsu (Japan)	1981 - Miss Z. Garrison (U.S.A.)	1993 - Miss N. Feber (Belgium)
1958 - Miss S. M. Moore (U.S.A.)	1970 - Miss S. Walsh (U.S.A.)	1982 - Miss C. Tanvier (France)	1994 - Miss M. Hingis (Switzerland)
1959 - Miss J. Cross (S.A.)	1971 - Miss M. Kroschina (U.S.S.R.)	1983 - Miss P. Paradis (France)	

GIRLS' DOUBLES

1982 - Miss B. Herr and Miss P. Barg	1987 - Miss N. Medvedeva and Miss N. Zvereva	1992 - Miss M. Avotins and Miss L. McShea
1983 - Miss P. Fendick and Miss P. Hy	1988 - Miss J. A. Faull and Miss R. McQuillan	1993 - Miss L. Courtois and Miss N. Feber
1984 - Miss C. Kuhlman and Miss S. Rehe	1989 - Miss J. Capriati and Miss M. McGrath	1994 - Miss E. De Villiers and Miss E. E. Jelfs
1985 - Miss L. Field and Miss J. Thompson	1990 - Miss K. Habsudova and Miss A. Strnadova	
1986 - Miss M. Jaggard and Miss L. O'Neill	1991 - Miss C. Barclay and Miss L. Zaltz